I0415722

Vegetation Classification and Mapping Project Report, Fort Larned National Historic Site

Natural Resource Technical Report NPS/SOPN/NRTR—2007/072

A Report for the Southern Plains Inventory and Monitoring Network

National Park Service
Southern Plains Inventory and Monitoring Network
P.O. Box 329 (mailing)
100 Ladybird Lane (physical)
Johnson City, TX 78636

Authors
Dan Cogan
Cogan Technology Inc.
21 Valley Road Galena, IL 61036

Lisa M. Castle Walker, Hillary Loring, Suneeti Jog, and Jennifer Delisle
Kansas Natural Heritage Inventory, Kansas Biological Survey
2102 Constant Ave. Lawrence, KS 66047

May 2007

U.S. Department of the Interior
National Park Service
Natural Resource Program Center
Fort Collins, Colorado

The Natural Resource Publication series addresses natural resource topics that are of interest and applicability to a broad readership in the National Park Service and to others in the management of natural resources, including the scientific community, the public, and the NPS conservation and environmental constituencies. Manuscripts are peer-reviewed to ensure that the information is scientifically credible, technically accurate, appropriately written for the intended audience, and is designed and published in a professional manner.

The Natural Resource Technical Reports series is used to disseminate the peer-reviewed results of scientific studies in the physical, biological, and social sciences for both the advancement of science and the achievement of the National Park Service's mission. The reports provide contributors with a forum for displaying comprehensive data that are often deleted from journals because of page limitations. Current examples of such reports include the results of research that addresses natural resource management issues; natural resource inventory and monitoring activities; resource assessment reports; scientific literature reviews; and peer reviewed proceedings of technical workshops, conferences, or symposia.

Views and conclusions in this report are those of the authors and do not necessarily reflect policies of the National Park Service. Mention of trade names or commercial products does not constitute endorsement or recommendation for use by the National Park Service.

Printed copies of reports in these series may be produced in a limited quantity and they are only available as long as the supply lasts. This report is also available from the Natural Resource Publications Management Website (http://www.nature.nps.gov/publications/NRPM) on the Internet, or by sending a request to the address on the back cover.

Please cite this publication as:

Cogan, D., L.Walker, H. Loring, S. Jog, and J Delisle. 2007. Vegetation Classification and Mapping Project Report, Fort Larned National Historic Site, National Park Service, Southern Plains Network. Natural Resource Technical Report NPS/SOPN/NRTR—2007/072. National Park Service, Fort Collins, Colorado. D-66

NPS D-66 May 2007

Contents

Page

Figures...4

Tables...4

List of Contacts and Contributors 5

Acknowledgements...6

List of Abbreviation and Acronyms 7

Links 7

Executive Summary 8

Project Statistics...10

Introduction..11

Method..17

Results...32

Discussion...40

Literature Cited 43

APPENDIX A: Components and Flow Diagram of the Vegetation Classification and Mapping Program 45

APPENDIX B: Field Data Forms and Instructions 46

APPENDIX C: Dichotomous Key to FOLS Plant Associations 64

APPENDIX D: Vegetation Association Descriptions for FOLS..............................66

APPENDIX E: FOLS Species List..87

APPENDIX F: Photo Interpretation Mapping Conventions and Visual Key............91

APPENDIX G: Final FOLS Vegetation Map...103

Figures

Figure 1. Map of SOPN showing the location of the park units in the network..........................15

Figure 2. Map of the vegetation project boundary and park boundaries 18

Figure 3. Location of all vegetation plots collected at FOLS in 2005...22

Figure 4. Location of all observation and incidental points collected at FOLS in 2006 23

Figure 5. Examples of the NAIP 2005 and the 2005 CIR imagery for Fort Larned...................25

Figure 6. Location of all accuracy assessment points collected at FOLS in 2006......................30

Tables

Table 1. Polygon attribute items and descriptions used in the FOLS GIS coverage 27

Table 2. Target number of AA samples per map class based on number of polygons and area .28

Table 3. Summary of the AA Statistics used at FOLS 31

Table 4. List of NVC Plant Associations and Alliances found at FOLS 33

Table 5. Map units identified in FOLS 34

Table 6. Total acreage and frequency of map units for FOLS..37

Table 7. Contingency table (error matrix) for vegetation mapping at FOLS 39

List of Contacts and Contributors

U. S. Department of the Interior - U. S. National Park Service

Karl Brown Ph. D.
Vegetation Mapping Program Manager
1201 Oakridge Drive, Suite 200
Fort Collins, CO 80525
Phone: 970-225-3591
Email: karl_brown@nps.gov

Dusty Perkins Ph. D.
S. Plains Network Coordinator
P.O. Box 329, 100 Ladybird Lane
Johnson City, TX 78636
Phone: 830-868-7128 ext. 281
Email: dustin_w_perkins@nps.gov

Felix Revello
FOLS Chief Ranger
RR3 Box 69
Larned, KS. 67550-9321
Phone: 620 285-6911
Email: felix_revello@nps.gov

Jim Drake - NatureServe
Regional Vegetation Ecologist
1101 West River Parkway Suite 200
Minneapolis, Minnesota 55415
Phone: 612-331-0729
E-mail: jim_drake@natureserve.org

Dan Cogan - Cogan Tech. Inc.
Scientist and GIS Specialist
21 Valley Road
Galena, IL 61036
Phone: 815-777-1773
E-mail: dancogan@cogantech.com

Kelly Kindscher - KSNHI
Community Ecologist
2102 Constant Ave.
Lawrence, KS 66047
Phone: 785-864-1500
E-mail: kindsche@ku.edu

U. S. Department of the Interior - United States Geological Survey - Biological Resources Division

Mike Mulligan
USGS Program Coordinator
USGS-Center for Biological Informatics (CBI)
Phone: 303-202-4242
E-mail: mike_mulligan@usgs.gov

Theresa Singh
Website and Data Manager
USGS-Center for Biological Informatics
Phone: 303-202-4227
E-mail: theresa_singh@usgs.gov

U. S. Department of the Interior - Bureau of Reclamation

Michael Pucherelli
Group Manager GIS / Remote Sensing Group
P.O. Box 25007 Mail Stop 86-68260
Denver Federal Center - Bldg. 56
Denver, CO 80225
Phone: 303-445-2267
E-mail: mpucherelli@do.usbr.gov

David E. Salas
Physical Scientist
Phone 303-445-3619
Fax: 303-445-6337
E-mail: desalas@do.usbr.gov

Others: **Heidi Sosinski** & **Tomye Folts-Zettner** - Southern Plains Network, and **Chris Lea** - NPS Botanist Vegetation Mapping Program.

Acknowledgements

This project directly reflects the tireless leadership and diligent efforts of Dusty Perkins, Heidi Sosinski and Tomye Folts-Zettner with the Southern Plains Inventory and Monitoring Network. Dusty was instrumental in kicking-off this project and I would like to personally thank him for believing in my work and helping me throughout. I would also like to acknowledge the GIS and imagery assistance provided by Heidi. Always positive, Heidi fielded my questions and always provided me with the answers that I needed in a timely manner. Finally Tomye has been a great asset helping out with collecting the field data and reviewing the project reports. In my opinion the parks in the SOPN are extremely fortunate to have these three extremely capable professionals.

Felix Revello and the staff at Fort Larned National Historic Site were excellent with which to work. Always professional and extremely helpful they provided great support in the field pointing out features and adding their support to the project. I'm also very grateful to for Felix's hospitality and his support. It was truly a pleasure to work with Felix and I really enjoyed spending time with him and experiencing his park.

I would like to give a big thank you to Kelly Kindscher, Lisa M. Castle Walker, Hillary Loring Suneeti Jong, and Jennifer Delisle with the Kansas Biological Survey (KBS) - Kansas Natural Heritage Inventory (KSNHI) for providing an extremely rich data-set of invaluable plot, accuracy assessment and photo verification data. Their professionalism, dedication, and ecological and botanical knowledge of the Kansas flora was integral to the data collection, analysis, report writing/reviewing, and implementation of the National Vegetation Classification System for FOLS. They were a pleasure to work with and without them this project would not have been possible. In addition to the field work, Kansas Biological Survey also acquired topnotch imagery for the project. I would like to thank Mike Houts and Bernadette Kuhn for their work on the imagery and for helping to manage all of the data.

I would like to acknowledge the assistance that my former colleagues provided at the BOR. A special thank you goes to David Salas who backed me up throughout the whole project by fielding questions and reviewing materials. Ron Miller was also a great help in the field and at the kick-off meeting. I would also like to thank Mike Pucherelli for his continued support on these projects and for his companionship on one of the first trips to FOLS.

Special recognition goes to Karl Brown, Mike Story and Chris Lea with NPS for making this project happen and being there for help with coordination, logistics, and financial matters.

Finally, let me conclude by apologizing to anyone I may have inadvertently left off this list. Please know that I had a great experience working and meeting with everyone associated with this endeavor and I really appreciate all the effort that went into this project.   - Dan.

List of Abbreviation and Acronyms

AA	Accuracy Assessment
AML	Arc Macro Language
BOR	Bureau of Reclamation (also USBR)
BRD	Biological Resource Division (of the USGS)
CBI	Center for Biological Informatics (of the USGS/BRD)
CIR	Color Infrared Imagery
CTI	Cogan Technology Inc.
FGDC	Federal Geographic Data Committee
FOLS	Fort Larned National Historic Site
FSA	Farm Service Agency
GIS	Geographic Information System(s)
GPS	Global Positioning System
KBS	Kansas Biological Survey
KSNHI	Kansas Natural Heritage Inventory
MMU	Minimum Mapping Unit
NAD	North American Datum
NAIP	National Agriculture Imagery Program
NBII	National Biological Information Infrastructure
NPS	U.S. National Park Service
NRCS	Natural Resources Conservation Service
NVC	National Vegetation Classification
NVCS	National Vegetation Classification System
RSGIG	Remote Sensing and Geographic Information Group
SOPN	Southern Plains Inventory and Monitoring Network
TNC	The Nature Conservancy
USBR	United States Bureau of Reclamation (also BOR)
USDA	United States Department of Agriculture
USGS	United States Geological Survey
UTM	Universal Transverse Mercator

Links

http://www.nature.nps.gov/im/units/sopn/index.cfm	Southern Plains Inventory and Monitoring Network
http://biology.usgs.gov/npsveg/index.html	USGS-NPS Vegetation Mapping Program
http://www.nps.gov	The National Park Service
http://usgs.gov	United States Geologic Survey
http://biology.usgs.gov/cbi	USGS Center for Biological Informatics
http://biology.usgs.gov/cbi/nbii	National Biological Information Infrastructure
http://www.nps.gov/fols	Fort Larned National Historic Site
http://www.usbr.gov	United States Bureau of Reclamation
http://www.natureserve.org	NatureServe
http://www.natureserve.org/explorer	NatureServe Explorer® online database server
http://www.ksnhi.ku.edu/index.htm	Kansas Natural Heritage Inventory
http://plants.usda.gov	NRCS PLANTS Database

Executive Summary

Fort Larned National Historic Site (FOLS) encompasses 705 acres across two sites in the central portion of Kansas just west of the town of Larned. These unique sites support over 240 species of plants and include many examples of native riparian vegetation and remnants of the tallgrass prairie plant communities indigenous to this area. The park consists of two districts -Fort Larned is the larger of the two and it preserves and commemorates the original buildings and fort grounds. The Santa Fe Ruts site is smaller and preserves some of the original wagon ruts left by the immigrants on the Santa Fe Trail. To better understand the distribution of the plant assemblages located on these sites, the NPS Southern Plains Inventory and Monitoring Network (SOPN) started a vegetation mapping and classification effort at FOLS in 2005.

A three-year program was initiated to complete the task of mapping and classifying the vegetation at FOLS. Phase one, directed by the Kansas National Heritage Inventory (KSNHI) in conjunction with NatureServe developed a vegetation classification using the National Vegetation Classification System (NVCS). Phase two, directed by the U.S. Bureau of Reclamation's (BOR) Remote Sensing and GIS group in conjunction with Cogan Technology, Inc (CTI) produced a digital vegetation map. To classify the vegetation, 61 representative plots located throughout the approximately 1,898 acre project area (parks + environs) were sampled during the summer of 2005. Analysis of the plot data by KSNHI produced 9 distinct plant associations and alliances, 1 of which was newly described in the NVCS. In addition, CTI described 2 more alliances (i.e. Park Specials) that primarily occurred as small stands or were located outside of the park boundary in the environs. Descriptions and a field key for all 11 unique plant assemblages for FOLS are included in this report.

To produce the digital map, a combination of 1:8,500-scale (0.75 meter pixels) color infrared digital ortho-imagery acquired on October 26, 2005 by the Kansas Applied Remote Sensing Program and 1:12,000-scale true color ortho-rectified imagery acquired in 2005 by the U.S. Department of Agriculture - Farm Service Agency's Aerial Photography Field Office, and all of the GPS referenced ground data were used to interpret the complex patterns of vegetation and land-use. In the end, 16 map units (11 vegetated and 5 land-use) were developed and directly cross-walked or matched to corresponding plant associations and land-use classes. All of the interpreted and remotely sensed data were converted to Geographic Information System (GIS) databases using ArcGIS© software. Draft maps were printed, field tested, reviewed and revised. One hundred and six accuracy assessment (AA) data points were collected in 2006 by KNSHI and used to determine the map's accuracy. After final revisions, the accuracy assessment revealed an overall thematic accuracy of 92%.

Products developed for Fort Larned National Historic Site are described and presented in this report, and are stored on the accompanying DVD. These include:

- A *Final Report* that includes keys to the vegetation and imagery signatures, AA information, and all of the methods and results of the project;
- A *Spatial GIS Database* containing spatial data for the vegetation, plots, and AA points;
- *Digital Photos* from sample plots and miscellaneous park views;
- *Metadata* for all spatial data [Federal Geographic Data Committee (FGDC-compliant];
- *Vegetation Descriptions and Photo Signature Key* to the map classes and associations/alliances.

In addition, FOLS and the SOPN both received copies of:
- Digital data files and hard copy data sheets of the observation points, vegetation field plots, and accuracy assessment points;
- Hardcopy vegetation maps.

Additional data not included in this report can be found on the attached DVD. These data include text and metadata files, keys, lists, field data, spatial data, the vegetation map, and ground photos. Please access the following USGS website for posting of this information: http://biology.usgs.gov/npsveg/index.html

For more information on the NVCS and NVC alliances/associations in the United States please visit NatureServe's website: http://www.natureserve.org.

A picture of some of the bunkhouses and parade grounds at FOLS.
Photograph by: KSNHI

Project Statistics

Field Work Summers of 2005 and 2006:

    Plot Sampling = 61 Plots:
        61 Plots Sampled in September and October of 2005 by Lisa Castle Walker with the
        Kansas National Heritage Inventory

    Accuracy Assessment Points = 106
        106 Points collected on October 3 - 6, 2006 by the Kansas National Heritage Inventory

Classification:

    5 NVC Plant Associations (including the Prairie Dog Town Grassland Complex)
    6 NVC Vegetation Alliances

GIS Database 2002-2005:

    Project Size = 1,898 acres
    Fort Larned National Historic Site (including the Rut Site) = 705 acres

    Base Imagery acquired from the USDA FSA Aerial Photography Field Office acquired
    through the National Agriculture Imagery Program:
        2005 - 1:12,000-scale true color ortho-rectified imagery, compressed county
        mosaic,2 meter pixel resolution.

    Ancillary Imagery acquired by the Kansas Applied Remote Sensing Program, a division
    of the Kansas Biological Survey:
        October 26, 2005 - 1:8,500-scale color infrared digital ortho-imagery,
        uncompressed, 0.75 meter pixel resolution.

    16 Map Classes
        11 Vegetated
        5 Non-vegetated

    Minimum Mapping Unit = ½ hectare is the program standard but this was modified at
        FOLS to ¼ acre.

    Total Size = 229 Polygons

    Average Polygon Size = 8.3 acres

    Overall Thematic Accuracy = 92%

    Project Completion Date: 05/31/07

Introduction

Background

In 1994, the U.S. Geological Survey (USGS) and NPS formed the USGS-NPS Vegetation Mapping Program to cooperatively inventory and map the vegetation in the United States National Parks. The goals of this program are to provide baseline ecological data for park resource managers, obtain data that can be examined in a regional and national context, and provide opportunities for future inventory, monitoring, and research activities (FGDC 1997, Grossman et al. 1998).

In the same year, the USGS-NPS Vegetation Mapping Program also adopted the U.S. National Vegetation Classification (USNVC) (The Nature Conservancy and Environmental Systems Research Institute 1994a, Grossman et al. 1998) as a basis for the *a priori* definition of vegetation units to be inventoried. The Federal Geographic Data Committee adopted a modified version of the upper (physiognomic) levels as a federal standard (FGDC-STD-005)(FGDC 1997). This standard was hereafter termed the National Vegetation Classification Standard (NVCS). The NVCS established a federal standard for a complete taxonomic treatment of vegetation in the United States at physiognomic levels. It also established conceptual taxonomic levels for the floristic units of alliance and association, largely following the USNVC, but did not offer a taxonomic treatment for the floristic levels because of the immense scope of establishing robust floristic units for the entire United States. The FGDC standard requires that federally funded vegetation classification efforts collect data in a manner that enables crosswalking the data to the NVCS (i.e., the physiognomic levels) and sharing between agencies, but does not require use of that standard by agencies for internal mission needs. NatureServe maintains a treatment of floristic units (alliances and associations), which, though not a federal standard, are used as classification and mapping units by the vegetation mapping program whenever feasible. For purposes of this document, the federal standard (FGDC 1997) is denoted as the NVCS; the USNVC will refer exclusively to NatureServe's treatment for vegetation floristic units (alliances and associations only).

Use of the NVCS as the standard vegetation classification system is central to fulfilling the goals of this national program. This system:

- is vegetation based;
- uses a systematic approach to classify a continuum;
- emphasizes natural and existing vegetation;
- uses a combined physiognomic-floristic hierarchy;
- identifies vegetation units based on both qualitative and quantitative data;
- is appropriate for mapping at multiple scales.

The use of the NVC and the USGS-NPS vegetation mapping protocols facilitate effective resource stewardship by ensuring compatibility and widespread use of the information throughout the NPS as well as by other federal and state agencies. These vegetation maps and associated information support a wide variety of resource assessment, park management, and planning needs. In addition they can be used to provide a structure for framing and answering critical scientific questions about vegetation communities and their relationship to environmental conditions and ecological processes across the landscape.

The NVC has primarily been developed and implemented by The Nature Conservancy (TNC) and the network of State Natural Heritage Programs over the past twenty years (TNC 1994a; Grossman et al. 1998). The NCV is currently supported and endorsed by multiple federal agencies, the FGDC, NatureServe, State Heritage Programs, and the Ecological Society of America. Refinements to the classification occur in the process of application, leading to ongoing proposed revisions that are reviewed both locally and nationally. TNC and NatureServe have made available a 2-volume publication presenting the standardized classification, providing a thorough introduction to the classification, its structure, and the list of vegetation types found across the United States as of April 1997 (Grossman et al. 1998). *Volume I: The National Vegetation Classification Standard* can be found on the Internet at: http://www.natureserve.org/publications/library.jsp.

NatureServe has since superseded Volume II of the publication (the classification listing), providing regular updates to ecological communities in the United States and Canada. This online database server, NatureServe Explorer®, can also be found on the Internet at: http://www.natureserve.org/explorer.

Fort Larned National Historic Site

Fort Larned National Historic Site (FOLS) lies on the wind swept plains of central Kansas. Located in the heart of Pawnee County, this unique site commemorates Fort Larned and the important role it played in helping the United States expand westward. Established in 1859, Fort Larned served as a base for the U.S. Army and over four companies of soldiers. Fort Larned helped protect travelers along the Santa Fe Trail and was used by the Bureau of Indian Affairs as an administration office. Authorized by Congress in 1964 and purchased by the National Park Service in 1966, FOLS continues to preserve and celebrate this great example of a settlement period fort and its unique history.

The staff at FOLS administers two separate units approximately 4.5 miles apart. Located about 6 miles west of Larned, Kansas, Fort Larned is the larger of the two, containing nine restored buildings that made up the barracks, commissary and officer's quarters. All of the buildings have been, or are undergoing extensive restoration to insure their period appearance, circa 1868. This site is relatively flat but does contain a large portion of the Pawnee River including oxbows and historic channels. It is this location next to a bend in the river that likely prompted building on this site as it provided some protection on three sides and contained access to water.

The Santa Fe Trail Ruts site is located southwest of Fort Larned and this 45 acre site preserves one of the last remnants of the Santa Fe Trail. It is here that wagon wheel depressions left by the thousands of early pioneers as they traveled across the vast prairie can be observed. Unlike most of the trail, this site was never tilled or plowed but was kept intact as a small pasture until the National Park Service acquired the property following the establishment of FOLS. A tall observation tower on the southern edge of the property provides remarkable views of the gently rolling terrain, the longitudinal depression of the trail ruts and the shallow depressions of a few old bison wallows.

Natural Setting

Fort Larned is located on the upper floodplain of the Pawnee River. Situated next to a historic oxbow lake and south of the active river channel, this site contains large, flat grasslands common to the Southern Plains region. Until recently these large fields were actively farmed and ranched, heavily influencing the composition of the vegetation. These rural activities resulting in large areas planted with non-native grasses such as smooth brome (*Bromus inermis*) and patches of weedy, early seral species consisting of annual forbs and grasses. Currently the staff at FOLS is actively restoring these areas to tallgrass prairie with the hopes of bringing back the vegetation to a more natural condition. Along with the old fields the park also maintains and mows the grasslands planted in and around the historic fort, picnic and parking areas. Bisecting these areas is the Pawnee River that meanders through the site from east to west providing riparian habitat for thick stands of deciduous trees and shrubs lining both banks of the river.

The Santa Fe Ruts site contains a few remnants of the original tallgrass prairie vegetation and is inhabited by a colony of black-tailed prairie dogs. This site also contains some small drainages that trend from the northeast to the west-central boundary. These low areas are mesic and are often completely saturated most of the year.

The landscape around FOLS is fragmented and primarily rural. Surrounding both sites are extensive agricultural lands that are actively farmed or used for pasture. These fields are accessed through a network of state, county and private roads.

Vegetation

The vegetation of FOLS contains a mix of common Southern Plains native plants and agriculture-influenced non-native species. The natural plant communities in the area are not well-described but appear to be separated into two broad groups of tallgrass prairie and riparian forests. The uplands are typically drier and occur on the gentle sloping to flat floodplain terraces and broad plains. These habitats support large expanses of grassland largely being restored to native tallgrass prairie including the seeding of big bluestem (*Andropogan gerardii*), Indiangrass (*Sorghastrum nutans*) and switchgrass (*Panicum virgatum*). At the Santa Fe Ruts site these tallgrass species are also present and are likely remnants from the original pre-settlement tallgrass prairie. In addition, this small site contains a very active black-tailed prairie dog colony that clips the vegetation and keeps it very short. Grazing also influences the species composition favoring plants that are unpalatable and low-growing. Typical plants include species such as yellow foxtail (*Setaria pumila*), prairie three-awn (*Aristida oligantha*), horseweed (*Conyza ramosissimum*), wood sorrel (*Oxalis dillenii*), and field bindweed (*Convolvulus arvensis*). Western wheatgrass (*Pascopyrum smithii*) is also found at FOLS in one small natural area south of the fort.

Unfortunately most of the grasslands in and around FOLS have been altered through historical plowing and seeding. Alteration is evidenced by the abundance of smooth brome, Johnsongrass (*Sorghum halepense*), and other introduced grasses and forbs. On the heavily disturbed sites such as recently flooded areas, non-native, early seral species are present. These include poison hemlock (*Conium maculatum*), Mexican firebush (*Kochia scoparia*), Japanese brome (*Bromus japonicus*), pale dock (*Rumex altissimus*), western ragweed (*Ambrosia psilostachya*) and cheatgrass (*Bromus tectorum*).

Riparian corridors associated with the Pawnee River are typically lush with multi-strata of deciduous vines, shrubs, and trees. Common species include eastern cottonwood (*Populus deltoides*), green ash (*Fraxinus pennsylvanica*), black willow (*Salix nigra*), boxelder (*Acer negundo*), and elms (*Ulmus* spp.). Shrubs at FOLS are mainly restricted to understory species in the riparian habitats and do not occur as discrete associations. American plum (*Prunus americana*) is probably the most common shrub at FOLS. Along with the riparian trees and shrubs this area also supports seasonal stands of smartweeds (*Polygonum lapathifolium* and *Polygonum bicorne*). This unique vegetation type is dynamic at Fort Larned and is likely a result of the damming and silting of the river below FOLS. Smartweeds form nearly homogenous stands in and along the Pawnee River bottom when the water level is low. They are also present as a permanent stand at the Ruts site where a small drainage has been impounded by the roadbed.

FOLS Vegetation Mapping Project

The specific decision to classify and map the vegetation at FOLS was made in response to guidelines set forth by the NPS Natural Resources Inventory and Monitoring Program and implemented by the SOPN. The SOPN consists of 11 National Park units spread across 5 states in the south central portion of the United States (Figure 1). This network of parks was formed to create and centralize much-needed information about the nature and status of selected biological resources occurring within park boundaries so as to be used for making management decisions, for scientific research, and for educating the public. One of the goals of this network is to provide baseline inventory information for resource management and to help monitor the health of park ecosystems. Stemming from this goal, developing a vegetation classification to the plant community level and associated GIS map and database for each park was viewed as a high priority.

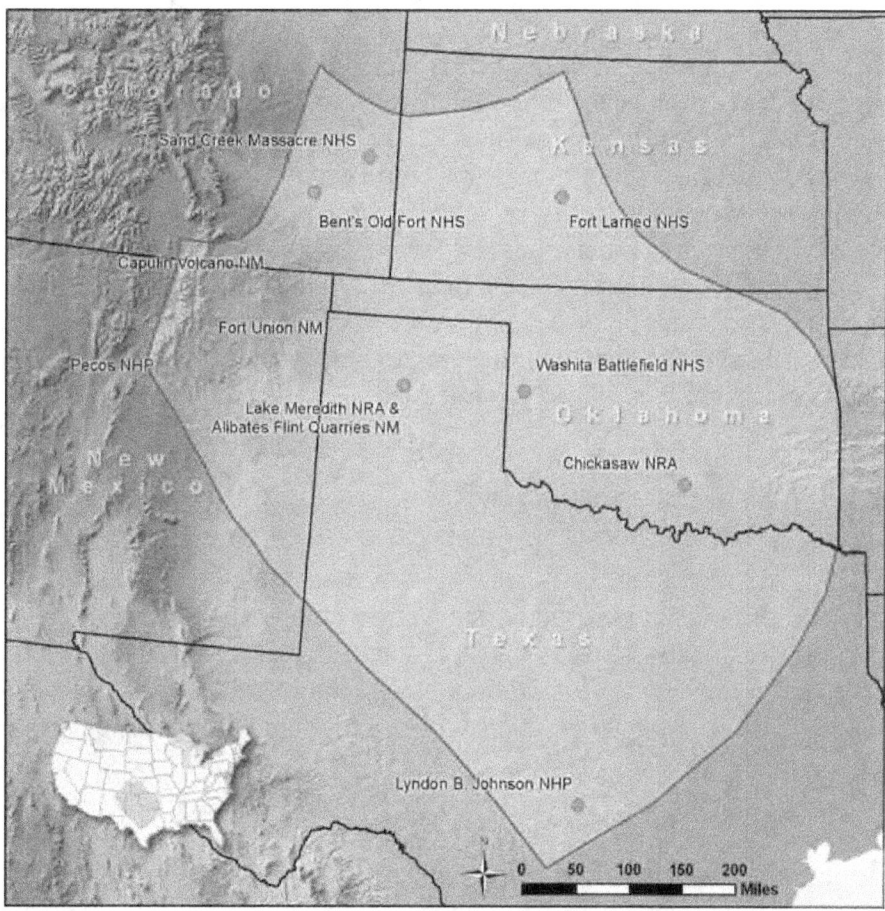

Figure 1. Map of SOPN showing the location of the park units in the network.

In 2005 Dusty Perkins, the network coordinator for SOPN at that time contacted the Bureau of Reclamation's Remote Sensing and Geographic Information Group (RSGIG) requesting a proposal for creating vegetation spatial databases for three park units in the SOPN. These parks included Fort Larned National Historic Site, Washita Battlefield National Historic Site, and Lyndon B. Johnson National Historical Park. In addition San Antonio Missions National Historical Park in the Gulf Coast Network (GULN) was added due to its close proximity to Lyndon B. Johnson National Historical Park. All four units totaled approximately 11,800 acres and included a 0.25-mile buffer into the surrounding environs. Upon acceptance of the RSGIG proposal, work was started by acquiring existing imagery and visiting the respective sites. In conjunction with the mapping portion, ecologists were contracted by SOPN to collect vegetation sample plots and observation points. These data were used by KSNHI to classify the vegetation to the association and alliance levels of the National Vegetation Classification System (NVCS). For FOLS the ecological sampling was also conducted by the KSNHI. After the project was started, Dan Cogan the principal investigator left the BOR to start his own company, Cogan Technology Inc (CTI). All of the subsequent mapping and GIS work was sub-contracted to CTI through existing contracts with Science Applications International Corp.

Together CTI, KSNHI, NatureServe, BOR, SOPN and FOLS formed a team, each responsible for a specific portion of the project as outlined in the program standards and flowchart provided by the Center for Biological Informatics (USGS/BRD) (**Appendix A**). KSNHI took the lead in collecting the standardized field samples and was responsible for entering this data into a digital database. KSHNI was tasked with classifying this data and providing a list and global descriptions for the FOLS plant associations. CTI and BOR were responsible for the imagery interpretation and creating a digital vegetation map and spatial database. SOPN and FOLS staff reviewed and evaluated the draft classification, wrote local vegetation descriptions for all associations, cross-walked associations to map classes, and wrote and field-tested the key to the vegetation classification. FOLS staff also provided logistical and technical support, and helped coordinate activities.

The objectives of this team were to produce final products consistent with the national program's mandates. These included:

- A Vegetation Classification based on the National Vegetation Classification System;
- A Map Unit Classification based on FOLS-specific requirements;
- A spatial database of FOLS's vegetation, using remote sensing and GIS techniques;
- Digital and hard copy vegetation maps with a minimum 80% accuracy per map class.

Scope of Work

Vegetation mapping for FOLS occurred within an approximate 1,898 acre project boundary. This area encompassed the authorized boundary of FOLS, the Santa Fe Trail Ruts site, and a general 0.25-mile environ radius. The final project area determination was based on management needs, financial constraints, and time limitations (Figure 2).

Methods

The vegetation mapping project at FOLS was considered to be in the "medium park" category based on the overall size of the project area (TNC 1994b). As such, the standard methodology for sampling and mapping is to visit the entire park and select representative sites. It is assumed that these sites will sufficiently characterize the vegetation types and explain their distribution across the park without having to survey each stand of vegetation. Based on this approach the assignment of responsibilities was divided into five major steps following the flowchart of major steps produced for the national program by the USGS (Appendix A). These responsibilities included the following:

1. Plan, gather data, and coordinate tasks;
2. Survey FOLS to understand and sample the vegetation;
3. Classify the vegetation using the field data to NVC standard associations and alliances and crosswalk these to recognizable map units;
4. Acquire current digital imagery and interpret the vegetation from these using the classification scheme and a map unit crosswalk;
5. Assess the accuracy of the final map product.

All protocols for this project as outlined in the following sections can be found in documents produced by The Nature Conservancy (1994a, 1994b, and 1994c) for the USGS-NPS Vegetation Mapping Program and are found at this website: http://biology.usgs.gov/npsveg.

Planning, Data Gathering and Coordination

A series of planning conference calls were held throughout 2005 attended by representative USGS, NPS, NatureServe, BOR, and SOPN staff. The goals of these calls were to (1) inform the SOPN/FOLS staff about the National Vegetation Mapping Program, (2) learn about the park's management issues and concerns, (3) review existing data, (4) develop a schedule and assign tasks, (5) get a commitment from SOPN/FOLS, (6) define possible cooperation with others, and (7) start defining a project boundary.

These calls in addition to follow-up meetings, conference calls and e-mails helped determine the project boundary and base imagery. As stated above, the final project boundary included both units of FOLS, and a modest ¼ mile environs (Figure 2). Once the boundary was finalized all of the latest NAIP imagery for this area was ordered from the USDA Geospatial Gateway website (http://datagateway.nrcs.usda.gov). Imagery included the county mosaics acquired in 2004

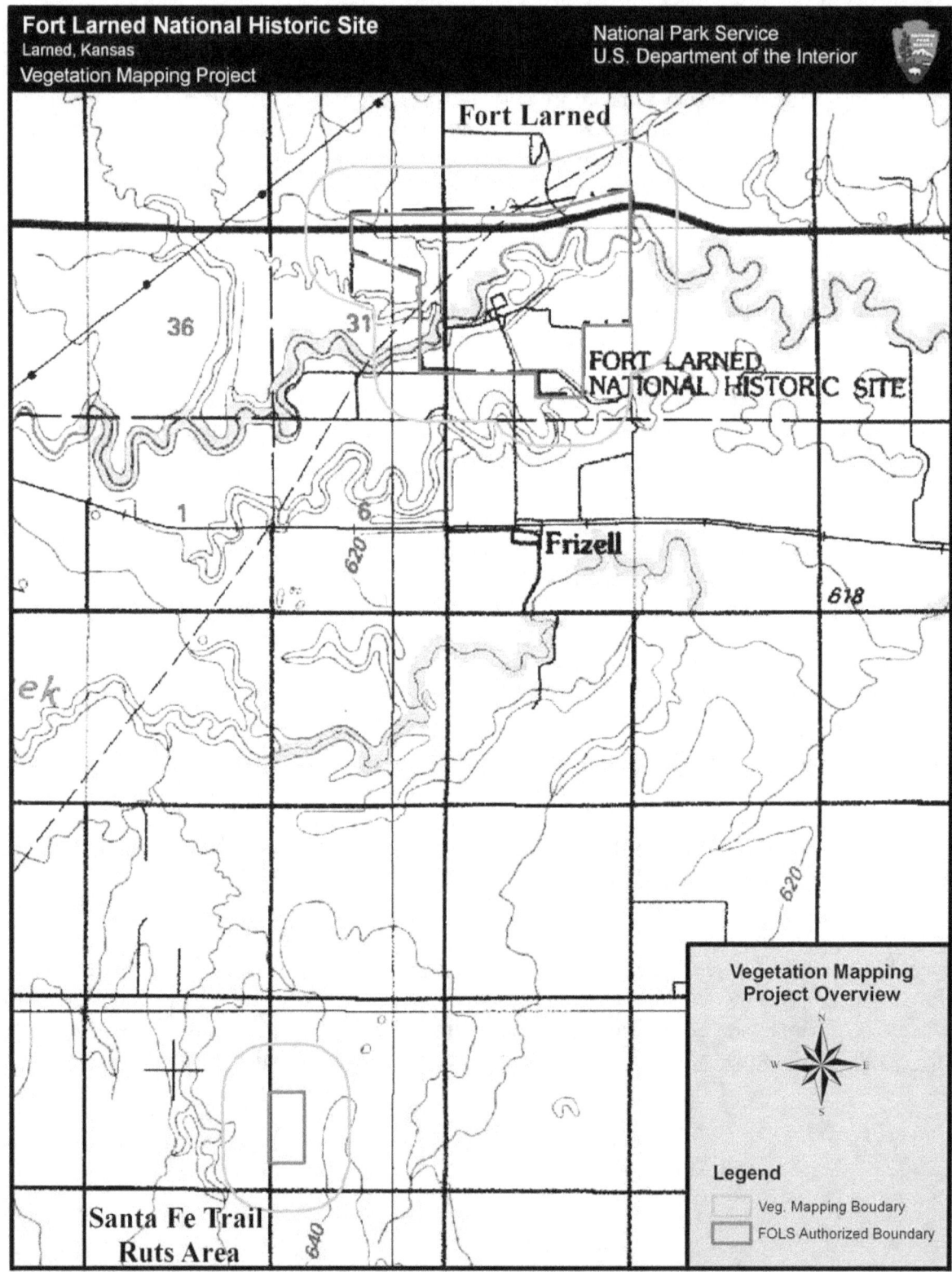

Figure 2. Map of the vegetation project boundary and park boundaries.

and 2005. All of the NAIP imagery was true color and had a 2-meter pixel resolution. Upon review by BOR and CTI, the 2004 imagery was not used for this project since it was slightly outdated. The 2005 imagery had 2-meter pixel resolution. In addition to the NAIP imagery, another set of color infrared imagery was acquired on October 26, 2005 by the Kansas Applied Remote Sensing Program. This imagery was acquired at 8,500 feet above ground level, for a resolution of approximately 0.75 meters. The resulting images were post processed, georeferenced, and then projected to UTM 14, NAD83 as a mosaiced, seamless image.

The remaining work responsibilities were assigned to the following participants:

FOLS-SOPN-NPS Responsibilities

- Provide oversight and project funding;
- Supply digital boundary files and ancillary data files;
- Assist with fieldwork and logistical considerations;
- Work with NatureServe to develop the vegetation classification;
- Compile, review, and update drafts of the vegetation map, classification and report;
- Accept the final products and close the project.

KSNHI Responsibilities

- Coordinate the field work with FOLS;
- Collect representative plot and accuracy assessment data;
- Collect less detailed observations about the draft vegetation map;
- Write a summary report.
- Work with NPS to develop a vegetation classification for the study area based on the NVC using quantitative analysis and ecological interpretation of the field data;
- Provide guidance regarding the crosswalk of vegetation types to map units;
- Provide global vegetation descriptions;
- Write a field key to the vegetation types.
-

CTI-BOR Responsibilities

- Help with overall project facilitation and coordination;
- Verify vegetation and land use/land cover signatures on the imagery;
- Develop map units linked to the NVC;
- Provide field maps and GIS support to the field crews;
- Interpret and delineate the final vegetation and land-use types;
- Transfer and automate interpreted data to a digital spatial database;
- Produce spatial layers of plot and accuracy assessment site locations;
- Assist with the accuracy assessment by picking the stratified random target points, creating field maps and providing GIS support;
- Provide a final report describing all aspects of the project;
- Provide a visual guide to the photo signatures of each map unit;
- Document FGDC-compliant metadata for all vegetation data;
- Create a DVD with reports, metadata, guides, vegetation classification, plot data, spatial data, the vegetation database (map), graphics, and ground photos.

Field Survey

Overall, the field methods used by the Kansas Natural Heritage Inventory in sampling and classifying the vegetation followed the methodology outlined by the USGS-BRD/NPS Vegetation Mapping Program and the NVC (Grossman et al. 1994, Grossman et al. 1998). The application of these methods to Fort Larned National Historic Site is outlined below.

At a scoping meeting in August 2005, KSNHI staff discussed strategies with FOLS and SOPN staff. At this meeting, preliminary basic classifications were proposed and special needs discussed. In addition to basic mapping and classification, FOLS staff had an additional goal of monitoring success in restoring smooth brome fields to tall grass prairie. To this end, transects of semi-permanent plots were positioned in fields at different stages of restoration.

Vegetation data were collected in "characteristic plots" and "transect plots." Upon first inspection, characteristic plots were located in areas that were visually representative of the preliminary vegetation categories. The first corner of a characteristic plot was positioned a given distance from a fixed point (e.g., 25 m from a fence post) or, where permanent structures were not close by, at a point in the characteristic vegetation where a GPS receiver's latitude and longitude last digits matched. Plots were then laid out following cardinal directions from the first point.

Transect plots were located at 30 m intervals along a measuring tape extended from a fixed point and marked with a metal stake driven into the ground at the corner. Plots in herbaceous vegetation were 100 m^2 and those in woody vegetation were 200 to 400 m^2. To maintain consistency with other projects in Kansas, plots were square except where the vegetation was in linear patches (wet swales and riparian stream banks), in which case the plots were rectangular. Plot locations were determined with a Garmin V GPS receiver set on recording the coordinates in NAD 27 CONUS (these were later re-projected by CTI to NAD 83 Conus). The accuracy for all of the recorded points ranged from 4-6 meters in horizontal accuracy, as recorded by the GPS receiver.

Where possible, three to five plots were sampled in each preliminary vegetation type with the following exceptions. Only one plot was taken in the poison hemlock vegetation and re-planted switchgrass vegetation since they were not found in enough places to allow for multiple plots. Also, the buffalo grass lawn type since it is an actively managed community was allotted one plot. Transects of three plots in restoration fields resulted in more than five plots in some preliminary vegetation categories.

All plants found within the plots were identified to species level where possible. In some cases, identification was only possible to the genus level (i.e., non-reproductive *Muhlenbergia* and *Carex* species). Visual estimates of percent cover were made for all species, including live material and the current year's standing dead (Daubenmire 1959). In order to maintain consistency with local vegetation surveys and other work of the KSNHI, a continuous range of possible cover estimates was used, rather than cover classes. Plants found to cover at least one half of one percent of the plot were assigned one percent (0.01) and those with less than one half of one percent a "trace" (T). Also to maintain consistency with published accounts and similar projects in the region, species were assigned names following the Flora of the Great Plains (1986). An updated synonymy was completed separately by Suneeti Jog of the KNSHI. Noteworthy surrounding vegetation, slopes, unusual soil features, and noticeable use by animals were also noted at each plot. Most of FOLS had been previously plowed for agriculture and many of the plots were on flat topography with an A horizon of silt and silty clay loam soils.

During the summer of 2006 a total of 67 plots were sampled across both units of the park (Figure 3) with eleven in primarily woody vegetation and fifty-six in herbaceous vegetation. Of these, 21 were laid out on transects and permanently marked to be used as references in measuring restoration success.

In addition to the sampling plots a number of observation points and incidental points were recorded in the field for signature verification purposes by CTI in 2006 before the accuracy assessment. A formal observation form was completed (Appendix B) for observation points. This form resembled the plot form except that the listing of all the species in the plot and their respective covers were omitted. An incidental point was simply a recording of the dominant vegetation and the Universal Transverse Mercator (UTM) NAD83 X-Y coordinates for its location. A total of 106 observation points and 24 incidental points were recorded at FOLS in 2006 (Figure 4).

Vegetation Classification

Upon completion of field surveys, all recorded data were entered into the NPS PLOTS database (TNC 1997), a MS Access-derived program. The PLOTS database was developed specifically for the NPS vegetation and mapping program so that the electronic data entry fields mirror the standard field form. Data entry was facilitated by assigning each plant taxon a unique, standardized code and name based on the PLANTS database developed by National Resources Conservation Service in cooperation with the Biota of North America Program (see website at http://plants.usda.gov). After data entry, checking was performed to minimize errors associated with duplicate entries or erroneously selected plant names. Problems regarding unknown species, especially those with high cover, were resolved, as were other taxonomic issues such as grouping some subspecies and varieties judged to be ecologically similar.

Plots were assigned to categories based on similarity of vegetation. These categories were assigned names following descriptions in Lauver et al. (1999) and NatureServe Explorer (NatureServe 2006). Where the observed FOLS vegetation did not fit descriptions of natural associations described for Kansas, semi-natural and disturbed associations or alliances described for other parks were considered. In several instances, the vegetation at FOLS had been planted with native species following years of agricultural use. These areas were assigned to the alliances of the dominant native species planted, with the addition of the term "Restored" even where the non-native species still dominate individual plots. In this manner, FOLS vegetation was assigned to one of ten plant associations and alliances. Once the associations were finalized, a dichotomous key was developed by KSNHI for use during the Accuracy Assessment (Appendix C). The full NVC hierarchical classification, global and local descriptions are available in Appendix D.

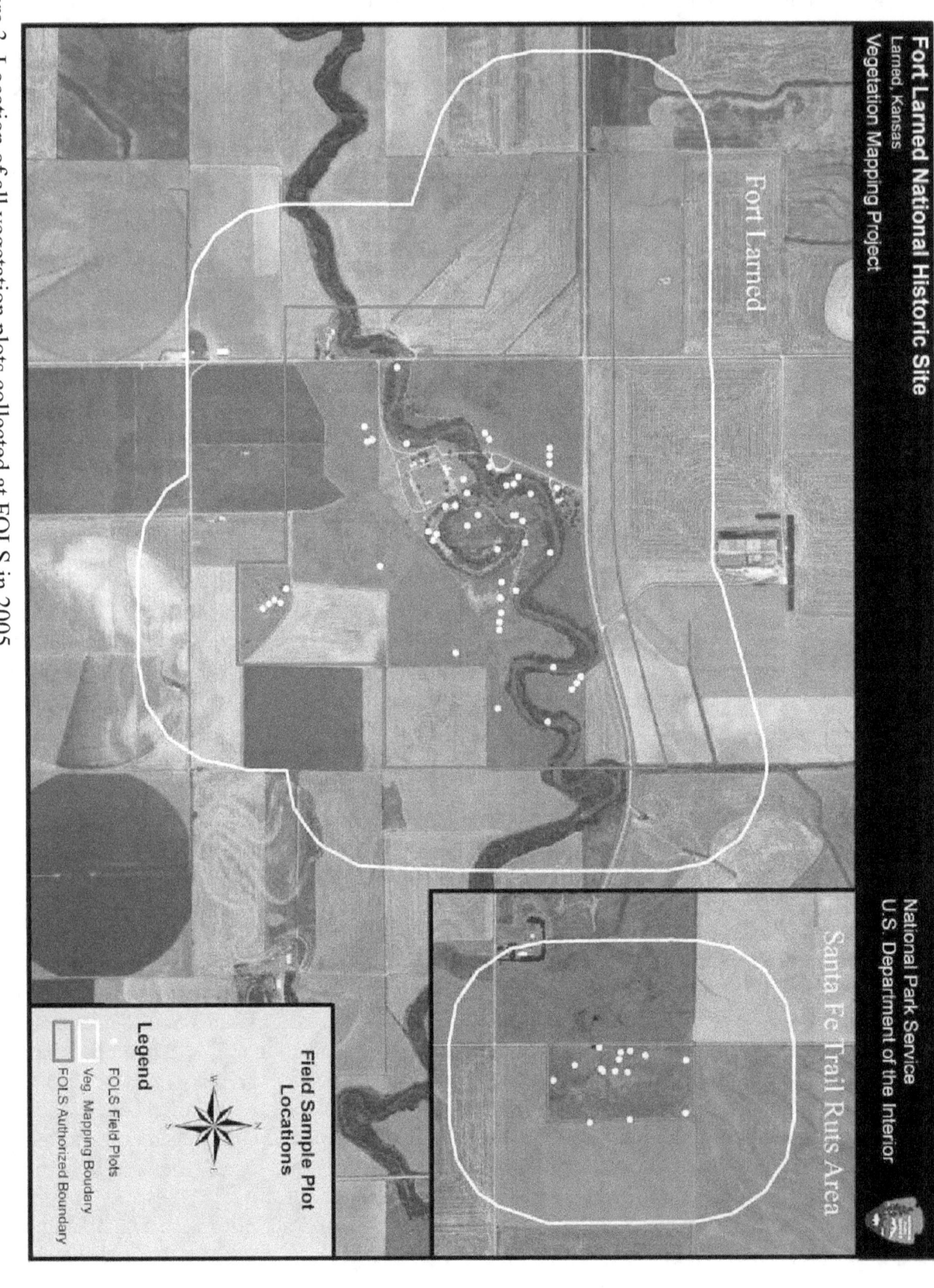

Figure 3. Location of all vegetation plots collected at FOLS in 2005.

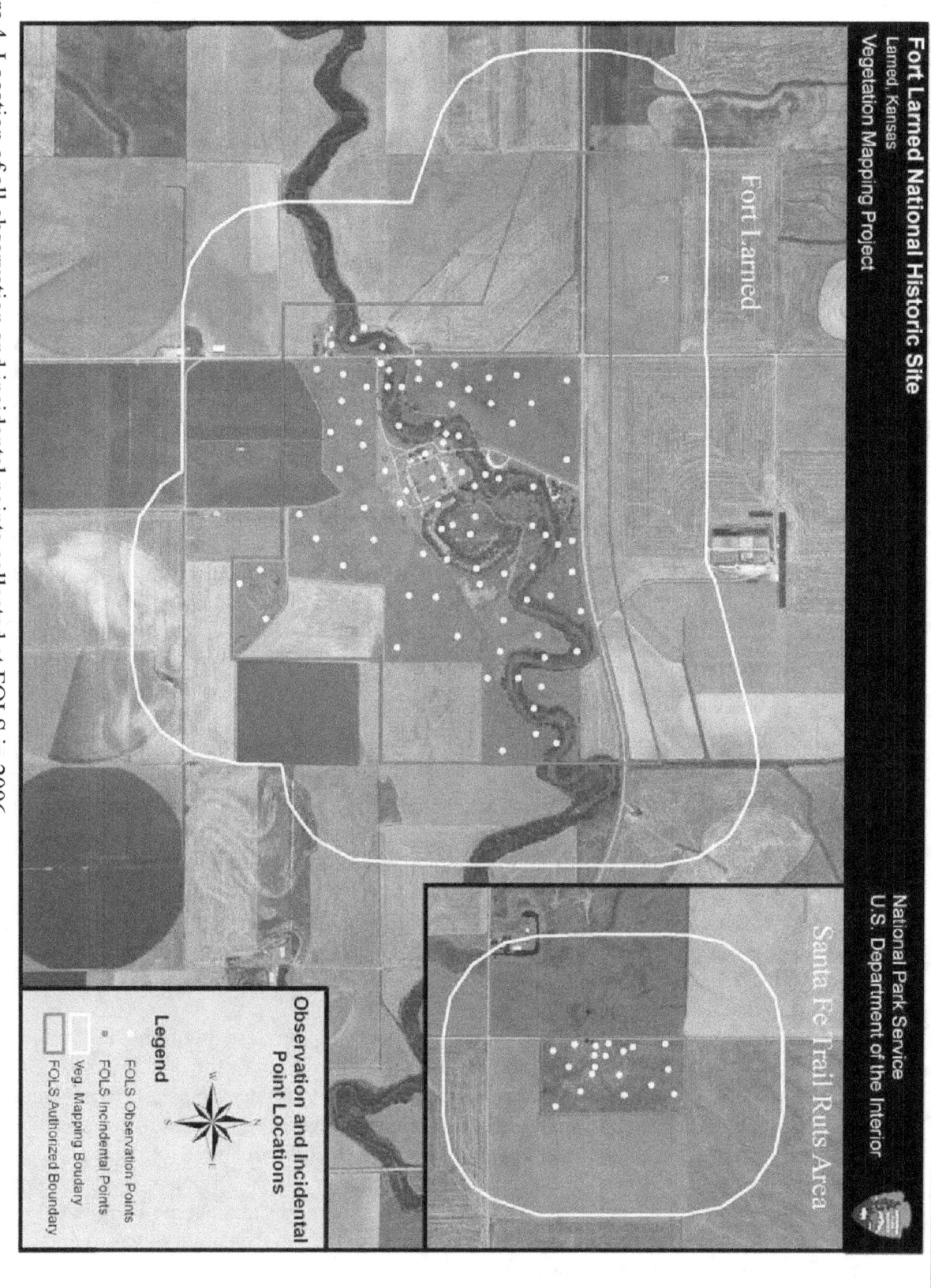

Figure 4. Location of all observation and incidental points collected at FOLS in 2006.

In addition, the final associations were linked to map classes for use in the photo-interpretation and mapping portions of the project.

In the future, FOLS classification plot data will be used by NatureServe and KSNHI to update and improve world-wide (i.e. global) descriptions of the NVC plant associations. FOLS specific (i.e. local) descriptions were written based on FOLS plot and AA data. The final FOLS classification contains 5 associations (including the Prairie Dog Town Grassland Complex) and 6 alliances.

Digital Imagery and Interpretation

After obtaining the NAIP 2005 imagery it was color balanced in Imagine Software by CTI to remove some of the edge-matching issues and sharpen the image. The resulting image was then mosaiced and clipped to just beyond the project boundary for both sites. Since the 2005 NAIP imagery was already available when the mapping started this was used as the basemap. once the CIR was delivered this was used as an ancillary base to map the grassland and deciduous tree vegetation (Figure 5).

Since the existing NAIP imagery for FOLS was true color the mapping team discussed acquiring additional color infrared imagery. Color infrared (CIR) imagery is often called false-color since the objects that are normally red appear green, green objects (except vegetation) appear blue, and "infrared" objects, which normally are not seen at all, appear red. Since healthy green vegetation is a very strong reflector of infrared radiation and appears bright red on color infrared photographs it helps tremendously in vegetation mapping efforts. Through the use of color infrared imagery subtle differences between cool and warm season grasses, wetland vegetation and deciduous tree are apparent and can be accurately delineated.

For FOLS, the Kansas Applied Remote Sensing Program, a division of the Kansas Biological Survey was contacted to acquire new CIR ortho-rectified imagery for both Fort Larned and the Santa Fe Ruts site. Upon agreement and funding from the National Park Service, the new imagery was acquired on October 26, 2005. Imagery was acquired from an altitude of 8500 above ground level, for a ground resolution of approximately 0.75 meters. A multispectral camera (DuncanTech MS3100) recorded data from the near infrared, red, and green wavelengths. Images were then post processed using ERDAS Imagine Photogrammetry Suite software and were georeferenced against a 2002 DOQQ. The resulting images were projected to the UTM 14, NAD83 projection and then mosaiced into a seamless image.

Interpretation of the vegetation at FOLS involved a three step process involving: (1) image segmentation, (2) cleaning and smoothing, and (3) ground-truthing of the data. First the 2005 NAIP imagery was re-sampled to a 3-meter pixel resolution to reduce noise and to generalize the vegetation signatures. Next this imagery was segmented using eCognition software to delineate obvious landforms (e.g. open water and fields) and physiognomic features (e.g. grasslands versus woodlands). The initial segments were created using a series of trial-and-error multi-resolution segmentation routines in the software. The settings for scale and shape were manipulated until a desired network of image objects resulted. The objective of the segmentation was to create a system of lines with as coarse a scale as possible without omitting most of the small, important and obvious land-cover patches. By iteratively increasing segmentation size within the program small image objects (i.e. preliminary polygons) were continuously merged into larger ones.

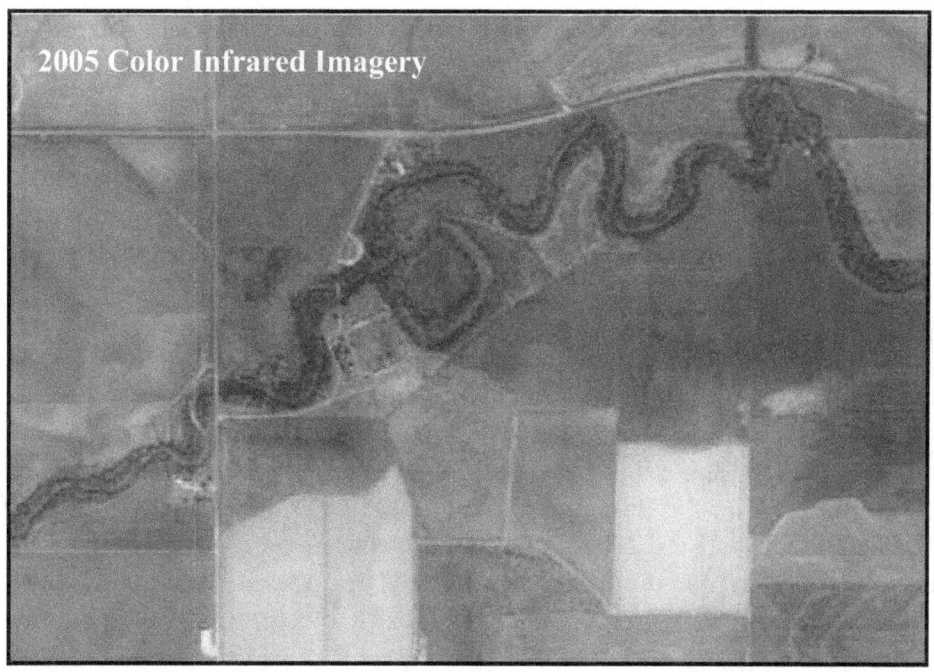

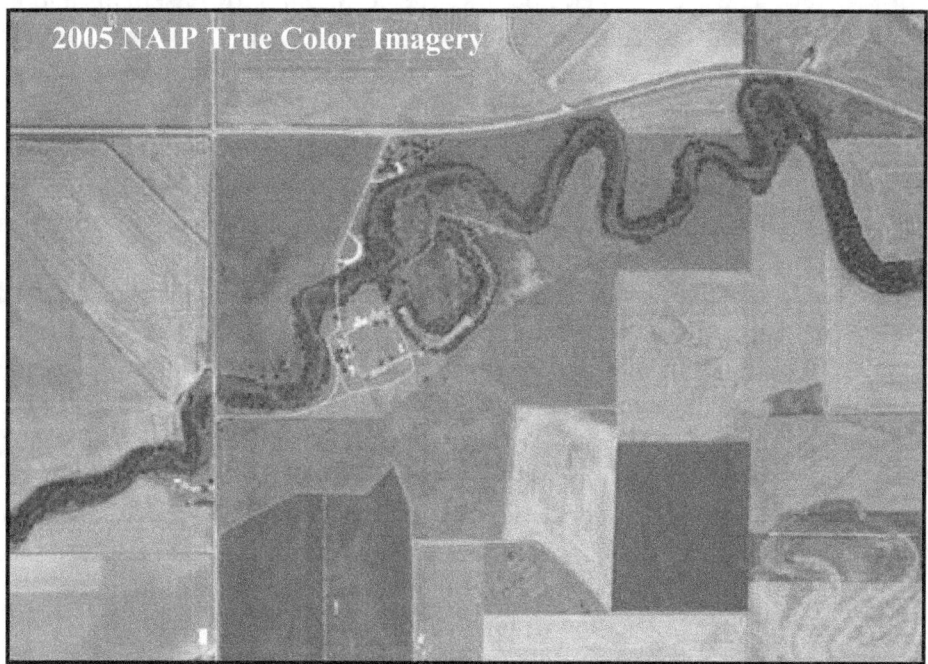

Figure 5. Examples of the NAIP 2005 and the 2005 CIR imagery for Fort Larned.

Completion of the segmentation was based on visual judgment of the analyst when obvious, distinct features were lost. At this point in the process the previous segmentation was adopted as the final treatment.

Following segmentation, the lines were exported as ArcInfo shapefiles and converted to ArcInfo coverages. The resulting coverages were run through a series of smoothing routines provided in the ArcGIS software. Smoothing was conducted to reduce the stair-stepping pattern of the lines resulting from the large pixels. Smoothing ended when no obvious artificial and relict breaks in the lines were visible. Following smoothing, the linework was manually cleaned to remove extraneous lines, small polygons, and polygons that obviously split a homogenous stand of vegetation. The cleaning stage was considered complete when all resulting polygons matched homogenous stands of vegetation apparent on the 2005 NAIP imagery

The lines resulting from the 2005 NAIP imagery segmentation were visually inspected in ArcInfo comparing them to the 2005 CIR imagery. Any obvious changes in the landscape between the two images were added or edited. Review of the merged polygon layer revealed that the roads and the facilities were not adequately separated from the surrounding vegetation. To resolve this, all large buildings, roads, streams and other linear and rectangular features were manually digitized directly off the 2005 NAIP imagery and incorporated into the final segmentation. After merging the digitized lines with the segmented linework the resulting preliminary GIS layer was considered complete and ready to be ground-truthed in the field.

Once the preliminary vegetation layer for FOLS was completed, 1:6,000-scale hard copy maps were printed for review. These contained both the true color and CIR basemaps and the linework as an overlay. During two days in 2006, researchers from CTI and BOR visited almost every polygon at both districts of FOLS. Ground-truthing consisted of verifying the maps against the actual vegetation on the ground to ensure that the polygons were labeled properly and to locate any extra or missing vegetation polygons. More general observations were also taken during this trip to help write descriptions for this report and create map units. All the information from this trip was subsequently added to the final GIS layer to correct any errors.

Upon return from the field, CTI researchers used the final NVC classification supplied by NatureServe to create map units. In most cases the map units were derived on a 1 association or alliance to 1 map unit basis. To round-out the mapping scheme, map units were created for land-use types based on a mapping system developed by Anderson et al. (1976). This system includes unvegetated lands not included in the NVC, such as roads, facilities, and agricultural fields. Finally a separate class of map modifiers or "Park Specials" was defined especially for FOLS to cover types that were not sampled or occurred outside of the park boundary. Park Specials included the western wheatgrass and Johnsongrass stands. In some cases NVC alliances were matched to the park specials. All of the resulting map unit names, map unit codes, NVC information, and other relevant attributes were added to each polygon in the GIS layer (Table 1).

Table 1. Polygon attribute items and descriptions used in the FOLS GIS coverage.

ATTRIBUTE	DESCRIPTION
AREA*	Surface area of the polygon in meters squared
PERIMETER*	Perimeter of the polygon in meters
FOLS_VEG#*	Unique code for each polygon
FOLS_VEG-ID*	Unique identification code for each polygon
MAP_CLASS	Final Map Unit Codes – Project specific
MAP_DESC	Map Unit Common Description Name – Project specific
DENS_MOD	Modifier - Percent cover of the upper stratum layer in the polygon
	Percent cover classes:
	Sparse = **10 - 25%,**
	Open = **25 - 60%,**
	Discontinuous - Closed = **> 60%**
PTRN_MOD	Modifier - Vegetation pattern within the polygon
	Vegetation pattern classes:
	Evenly Dispersed = **Homogeneous, Alternating,**
	Grouped Stands of Vegetation = **Bunched / Clumped,**
	String of Vegetation = **Linear**
HT_MOD	Modifier - Height range of the dominant vegetation layer
	Height classes: **0-0.5, 0.5-1, 1-5, 5-15, 15-30 meters**
DOM_MOD	Modifier – Dominant Herbaceous Species Observed in the Planted Semi – Natural Restored Grassland Prairie Map Class
CES_CODE	Ecological Systems Code – NVC derived (NatureServe)
CES_NAME	Ecological Systems Name – NVC derived (NatureServe)
IDENTIFIER	Corresponding Association or Alliance Name Code – NVC derived (NatureServe)
	Association = Community Element Global Code – Elcode link to the NVC
	Alliance = Alliance Global Code – Alliance Link to the NVC
ASSN_NAME	Project Community Name - NVC Association(s)
ASSN_CNAME	Project Common Community Name - synonym name of Association(s)
NVCS_CODE	NVC Code - to NVC Formation level
ALL_NAME	Project Alliance Name = NVC Alliance(s)
ALL_CNAME	Project Common Alliance Name = NVC Alliance(s)
FORMATION	NVC Formation = Formation name NVC Code – Formation name
SUBGROUP	NVC Formation Subgroup = NVC Code – Subgroup name
GROUP	NVC Formation Group = NVC Code – Group name
SUBCLASS	NVC Formation Subclass = NVC Code – Subclass name
CLASS	Formation Class = NVC Code – Class name
LUC_II_GEN	General Land Use and Land Cover Classification System Name – Project specific based on Level II of Anderson et al. (1976)
LUC_II	Specific Land Use and Land Cover Classification System Name
COMMENTS	General comments about the vegetation in the polygon
ACRES	Surface area of the polygon in acres
(*ArcInfo© default items)	

Accuracy Assessment

Once the vegetation layer was finalized the accuracy assessment (AA) was conducted. Typically in mapping exercises both thematic or attribute map accuracy as well as the positional or polygon line accuracy are considered. In the case of the USGS-NPS National Vegetation Mapping Program however, the positional accuracy is usually omitted since rarely does vegetation split on discrete edges that can be positively located in the field. The subjectivity involved in this effort plus the high resolution and accuracy of the NAIP and CIR basemaps usually allows for the assumption that all products derived from them are well within National Map Accuracy Standards for 1:12,000-scale maps (±30 feet). Further since no additional funding was budgeted or available the positional accuracy was not assessed.

The thematic accuracy of the vegetation map was assessed using the methodology following the standards provided by the USGS-NPS National Vegetation Mapping Program's Accuracy Assessment Procedures manual (TNC 1994c). Assessment included a four step process consisting of a sample design, sample site selection, data collection and data analysis. The design of the AA process followed the five possible scenarios provided in the field manual with stratified random targets placed in each map class based on their respective frequency and abundance (Table 2).

Table 2. Target number of AA samples per map class based on number of polygons and area.

Scenario	Description	Polygons in class	Area occupied by class	Recommended number of samples in class
Scenario A:	The class is abundant. It covers more than 50 hectares of the total area and consists of at least 30 polygons. In this case, the recommended sample size is 30.	> 30	> 50 ha	30
Scenario B:	The class is relatively abundant. It covers more than 50 hectares of the total area but consists of fewer than 30 polygons. In this case, the recommended sample size is 20. The rationale for reducing the sample size for this type of class is that sample sites are more difficult to find because of the lower frequency of the class.	< 30	> 50 ha	20
Scenario C:	The class is relatively rare. It covers less than 50 hectares of the total area but consists of more than 30 polygons. In this case, the recommended sample size is 20. The rationale for reducing the sample size is that the class occupies a small area. At the same time, however, the class consists of a considerable number of distinct polygons that are possibly widely distributed. The number of samples therefore remains relatively high because of the high frequency of the class.	> 30	< 50 ha	20
Scenario D:	The class is rare. It has more than 5 but fewer than 30 polygons and covers less than 50 hectares of the area. In this case, the recommended number of samples is 5. The rationale for reducing the sample size is that the class consists of small polygons and the frequency of the polygons is low. Specifying more than 5 sample sites will therefore probably result in multiple sample sites within the same (small) polygon. Collecting 5 sample sites will allow an accuracy estimate to be computed, although it will not be very precise.	5-30	<50 ha	5
Scenario E:	The class is very rare. It has fewer than 5 polygons and occupies less than 50 hectares of the total area. In this case, it is recommended that the existence of the class be confirmed by a visit to each sample site. The rationale for the recommendation is that with fewer than 5 sample sites (assuming 1 site per polygon) no estimate of level of confidence can be established for the sample (the existence of the class can only be confirmed through field checking).	< 5	< 50 ha	Visit all and confirm

These parameters were loaded into a custom GIS program along with the vegetation layer. The GIS program picked the random target locations and also buffered them 10 meters away from any polygon boundary and 50 meters away from any other point. Being able to choose minimum distance to polygon boundaries helped to minimize confusion and accounted for the horizontal error typically encountered in common GPS receivers (±5 m). The resulting target locations were restricted to only within the authorized boundaries of FOLS due to private land access constraints.

Once the target locations were selected they were sent to KSHNI. The electronic files were downloaded to Garmin GPS receivers and investigators walked to the AA points to complete the assessment. During the course of the field work, the estimated position error readings on GPS receivers ranged from 2-9 meters. KSNHI botanists were also provided with draft field maps, overview maps, map unit definitions, and a key to the associations and alliances (Appendix C). From October 3 - 6, 2006 KSNHI botanists traveled to 106 AA target sites and determined the vegetation association using the field key. At each target they recorded vegetation data on an AA form designed after one used for Thomas Stone NHS, a small park in Maryland. They also recorded height and cover of vegetative strata, environmental data, and percent canopy cover of the major species (see AA point form in Appendix B). Other nearby vegetation types outside of a 50-meter radius were also recorded as a mosaic component or as a co-dominant in a complex. A rationale for the choice of dominant association was noted when the decision was not clear cut.

During 2006 a total of 106 AA points were sampled (Figure 6). The data recorded on the field forms were subsequently entered into the PLOTS database and reviewed for data entry errors by KSHNI staff. Incomplete data on the field sheets were corrected if possible. The results were imported from the database into a GIS layer where they were visually compared in two stages to the vegetation map coverage. The first step was to compare the AA points to the original target locations to check for erroneous points and remove these from further analysis. General errors in the data were recorded at this time, including documenting points that had GPS and location errors. The most common GPS receiver error included transposing two UTM coordinate numbers. Location errors involved having the final AA point occur in the wrong target polygon either due to bad GPS satellite positioning or the point occurred too close to a polygon boundary. Through this process UTM coordinates for two points were corrected and one point was removed since it was located in the wrong target polygon likely caused by poor GPS receiver accuracy.

The second review step involved deciding between the primary and secondary call for the plant association as recorded by the field crew. In larger vegetation mapping projects such as Rocky Mountain National Park (Salas et al. 2004), AA analysis has involved fuzzy logic which assigns different levels of accuracy based on the primary, secondary and sometimes even the tertiary calls. However due to the small size of this project and the confusion that fuzzy logic can cause for the end user, a simple binary assessment was conducted. To accomplish this, CTI assigned a final map unit for every point by choosing between the primary and secondary calls. This was accomplished by first adding a new attribute to the AA point layer labeled "Final_Code" and then by comparing the assigned field names of the point with its corresponding location on the digital imagery. In most cases the primary vegetation map unit name assigned by the field crew was used. However some points were assigned their secondary field call based on one of the

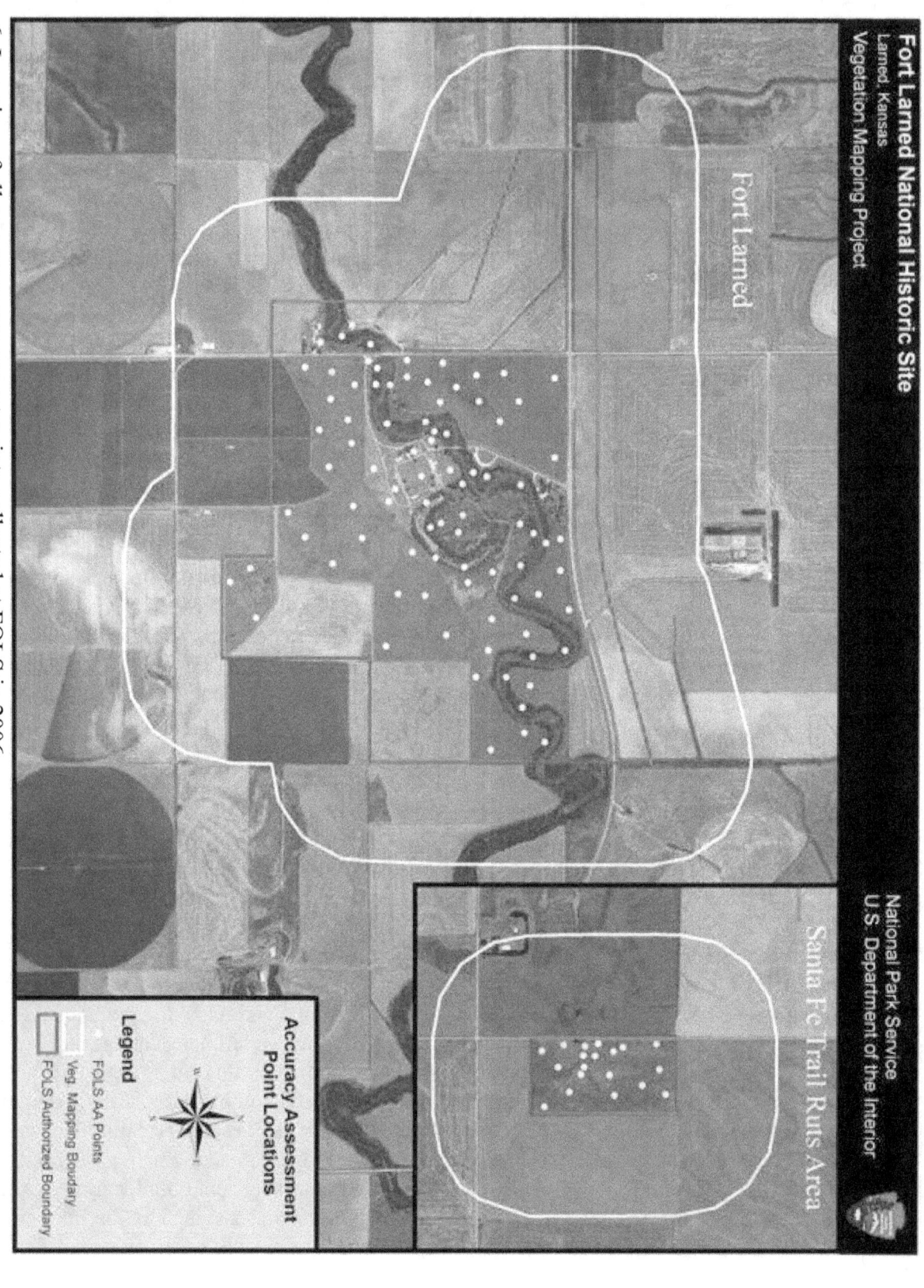

Figure 6. Location of all accuracy assessment points collected at FOLS in 2006.

following reasons: (1) it appeared that the second call was the better choice due to the overhead perspective (e.g. a stand judged to be sparse woodland on the imagery vs. called herbaceous vegetation in the field), (2) the data were actually recorded in a stand that was too small (i.e. inclusion), or (3) the second call better matched the ecological context (e.g. riparian woodland located next to a stream vs. upland woodland located next to a stream). Overall, roughly 10-20 points were reassigned to their secondary field call instead of the primary identification.

Once the data were reviewed the accuracy analysis was conducted. In the case of FOLS, the AA process was streamlined using methods developed from previous studies at Rocky Mountain National Park (Salas et al. 2004) and Wupatki National Monument (Hansen et al. 2004). Specifically many of the in-house GIS programs developed for these projects were used to compare the AA data, generate confidence intervals, Kappa statistics, and error matrices (contingency tables). Through this automated process, the final map unit in the AA layer was compared to the map unit designation for its corresponding polygon. All of the statistics and calculations used to analyze these data are described at length in the program manuals (TNC 1994c) and are summarized in Table 3. Final assessments for each point were recorded using an error matrix.

Table 3. Summary of the AA Statistics used at FOLS.

Statistic	Formula	Description
User's - accuracy:	$\dfrac{n_{ii}}{n_{i+}}$	Where i is the land cover type, n_{ii} is the number of matches between map and reference data and n_{i+} is the total number of samples of i in the map. This formula is the number of "correct" observations divided by the sum of the row.
Producer's accuracy	$\dfrac{n_{ii}}{n_{+i}}$	Where n_{+i} = total number of sample of i in the reference data. This formula is the number of "correct" observations divided by the sum of the column.
Confidence Interval	$\hat{p} \pm \left\{ z_\alpha \sqrt{\dfrac{\hat{p}(1-\hat{p})}{n}} + \dfrac{1}{(2n)} \right\}$	Where $z_\alpha = 1.645$ (this comes from a table of the z-distribution at the significance level for a two-sided limit with a 90% confidence interval). The term $1/(2n)$ is the correction for continuity. The correction should be applied to account for the fact the binomial distribution describes discrete populations $\hat{p}$ = the sample accuracy (0 -1.0), n = the number of sites sampled
Kappa Index	$k = \dfrac{N\sum\limits_{i=1}^{r} x_{ii} - \sum\limits_{i=1}^{r}(x_{i+} \times x_{+i})}{N^2 - \sum(x_{i+} \times x_{+i})}$	Where N is the total number of sites in the matrix, r is the number of rows in the matrix, x_{ii} is the number in row i and column i, x_{+i} is the total for row i, and x_{i+} is the total for column I.

Results

Vegetation Classification

The final classification for FOLS resulted in 5 associations and 6 alliances, 1 of which was newly described in the NVC (Old Field Weedy Herbaceous Vegetation). Two of the alliances were not sampled but were added by CTI as Park Specials during their verification efforts. The classification results reflect both the moderate amount of diversity of vegetation in the park and a respectably high number of native species. Table 4 contains the complete list of FOLS plant associations and alliances that were described in this study and Appendix D provides complete descriptions for each classification unit. During the sampling efforts a total of 145 species were recorded (Appendix E).

Digital Imagery and Interpretation

For FOLS, 16 map units were developed and directly cross-walked or matched to corresponding plant associations and land-use classes (Table 5). The types included 11 vegetation based map units and 5 land use classes. All of the vegetation units had a direct 1 map unit to 1 NVC association/alliance relationship. Please reference Appendix F for detailed descriptions and representative photos for all vegetation map units.

Relationship between Map Units and Plant Associations/Alliances
The FOLS map units represent a compromise between the detail of the NVC, the needs of the park and the limitations of the imagery. As a result, the mapping scheme is slightly different than the NVC. Vegetation map units are linked (i.e. "crosswalked") to the NVC plant associations or alliances when possible. When the NVC link was not feasible other map units were created. The only difference in the two classifications for FOLS is the use of the *Andropogon gerardii - (Sorghastrum nutans)* Herbaceous Alliance as the map class name instead of Planted Semi - Natural Restored Grassland Prairie.

The following were the possible map scenarios that were encountered at FOLS: (1) when a plant association or alliance had a unique photo signature and could be readily delineated on the photos, the map unit adopted the plant association/alliance name. This was considered a one-to-one relationship. (2) When unique stands of vegetation did not have a corresponding NVC association or alliance these were considered "park specials". (3) Finally, non-vegetated areas and vegetation types not recognized by the NVC received Anderson et al. (1976) Land Use – Land Cover map unit designations.

Table 4. List of NVC Plant Associations and Alliances found at FOLS.

Scientific Name	Common Name	Elcode[1]
Forest and Woodlands		
Populus deltoides - Salix nigra Forest	Eastern Cottonwood - Black Willow Forest	CEGL002018
Fraxinus pennsylvanica - Ulmus spp. - Celtis occidentalis Forest	Green Ash - Elm - Common Hackberry Forest	CEGL002014
Herbaceous Vegetation		
Andropogon gerardii - Sorghastrum nutans Western Great Plains Herbaceous Vegetation	Big Bluestem – Yellow Indiangrass Western Great Plains Herbaceous Vegetation	CEGL001464
Buchloe dactyloides Planted/Cultivated Herbaceous Vegetation	Buffalo Grass Lawn	A.1276
Prairie Dog Town Grassland Complex	Prairie Dog Town Grassland Complex	(No Assigned Code)
Andropogon gerardii - (Sorghastrum nutans) Herbaceous Alliance	Planted Semi - Natural Restored Grassland Prairie	A.1192
Old Field Weedy Herbaceous Vegetation	Old Field Weedy Herbaceous Vegetation	CEGL00XXXX
Bromus inermis Semi-natural Herbaceous Alliance	Smooth Brome Semi-Natural Herbaceous Alliance	A.3561
Hydrologically Disturbed Seasonal Polygonum spp. Vegetation	Smartweed species Seasonally Flooded Herbaceous Alliance	A.1881
*Pascopyrum smithii Herbaceous Alliance	Western Wheatgrass Herbaceous Alliance	A.1232
*Sorghum halepense Herbaceous Alliance	Johnsongrass Herbaceous Alliance	A.2020

*Represents discrete stands of vegetation that were not sampled either due to their small size or they occurred outside of the park boundary.

[1] ELCODE represents NatureServe's internal database tracking code for each recognized plant association or alliance.

Table 5. Map units identified in FOLS.

The units are organized into ecological groups. "Level" refers to whether the map unit represents a NVC plant association/alliance (NVC unless otherwise noted) or a local plant community/plant population (Park Special), or a land use class. Anderson Land Use Classes are identified by Roman numerals.

Map Code	Map Unit Name	Map Unit Common Name	Level
	Forest and Woodlands		
F-CTBW	*Populus deltoides - Salix nigra* Forest	Eastern Cottonwood - Black Willow Forest	Association
F-GASH	*Fraxinus pennsylvanica - Ulmus* spp. - *Celtis occidentalis* Forest	Green Ash - Elm - Common Hackberry Forest	Association
	Herbaceous Vegetation		
H-BIGB	*Andropogon gerardii - Sorghastrum nutans* Western Great Plains Herbaceous Vegetation	Big Bluestem – Yellow Indiangrass Western Great Plains Herbaceous Vegetation	Association
H-BUFO	*Buchloe dactyloides* Planted/Cultivated Herbaceous Vegetation	Buffalo Grass Herbaceous Alliance	Alliance
H-PDOG	Prairie Dog Town Grassland Complex	Prairie Dog Town Grassland Complex	Complex
H-REPR	*Andropogon gerardii - (Sorghastrum nutans)* Herbaceous Alliance	Planted Semi - Natural Restored Grassland Prairie	Association
H-OFLD	Old Field Weedy Herbaceous Vegetation	Old Field Weedy Herbaceous Vegetation	Alliance
H-SMBR	*Bromus inermis* Semi-natural Herbaceous Alliance	Smooth Brome Semi-Natural Herbaceous Alliance	Alliance
H-SMRT	Hydrologically Disturbed Seasonal *Polygonum* spp. Vegetation	Smartweed species Seasonally Flooded Herbaceous Alliance	Alliance
H-WTWG	*Pascopyrum smithii* Herbaceous Alliance	Western Wheatgrass Herbaceous Alliance	Alliance
H-JOHN	*Sorghum halepense* Herbaceous Alliance	Johnsongrass Herbaceous Alliance	Alliance
	Land Use – Land Cover		
L-STRM	(No Scientific Name)	Stream / River	Level III
L-AGRI	(No Scientific Name)	Agricultural Business	Level III
L-ROAD	(No Scientific Name)	Transportation	Level III
L-FACL	(No Scientific Name)	Park Facilities	N/A
L-FILD	(No Scientific Name)	Planted / Cultivated	Level III

*Park Special: Represents discrete stands of vegetation that were not sampled but classified based on field observations.

Below is a comprehensive breakdown of the crosswalking of the NVC associations to the map units for FOLS:

-Map Units Representing Single NVC Units (either existing or new)
(One Alliance/Association-to-One Map Class)

The following map units were created from the NVC and represent established or provisional plant alliances that could be discerned and delineated on the imagery.

Map Code	Map Unit *NVC Plant Alliance / Association(s)*
F-CTBW	*Populus deltoides - Salix nigra* Forest *Populus deltoides - Salix nigra* Forest
F-GASH	*Fraxinus pennsylvanica - Ulmus* spp. *- Celtis occidentalis* Forest *Fraxinus pennsylvanica - Ulmus* spp. *- Celtis occidentalis* Forest
H-BIGB	*Andropogon gerardii - Sorghastrum nutans* Western Great Plains Herbaceous Vegetation *Andropogon gerardii - Sorghastrum nutans* Western Great Plains Herbaceous Vegetation
H-BUFO	*Buchloe dactyloides* Planted/Cultivated Herbaceous Vegetation *Buchloe dactyloides* Planted/Cultivated Herbaceous Vegetation
H-PDOG	Prairie Dog Town Grassland Complex Prairie Dog Town Grassland Complex
H-OFLD	Old Field Weedy Herbaceous Vegetation Old Field Weedy Herbaceous Vegetation
H-SMBR	*Bromus inermis* Semi-natural Herbaceous Alliance *Bromus inermis* Semi-natural Herbaceous Alliance
H-SMRT	Hydrologically Disturbed Seasonal *Polygonum* Vegetation Hydrologically Disturbed Seasonal *Polygonum* spp. Vegetation
H-WTWG	*Pascopyrum smithii* Herbaceous Alliance *Pascopyrum smithii* Herbaceous Alliance
H-JOHN	*Sorghum halepense* Herbaceous Alliance *Sorghum halepense* Herbaceous Alliance

-Local Map Units Representing NVC Alliances

In cases when a NVC type had a corresponding NVC alliance these were named by the official NVC alliance name.

Map Code	Map Unit NVC Plant Alliance / Association(s)
H-REPR	*Andropogon gerardii - (Sorghastrum nutans)* Herbaceous Planted Semi - Natural Restored Grassland Prairie

Vegetation Map

Just over 1,898 acres including 705 acres in the authorized boundary of FOLS and an additional 1,193 acres in the environs were mapped using 16 map classes. This included 5 land cover classes and 11 vegetation classes. Of all the map units, the most frequent was *Bromus inermis* Semi-natural Herbaceous Alliance with 51 polygons. The most abundant map unit in terms of area other than the Planted/Cultivated fields in the environs was *Andropogon gerardii - (Sorghastrum nutans)* Herbaceous Alliance (Planted Semi - Natural Restored Grassland Prairie) covering 200 acres (80 hectares) or about 10% of the project area. All of the frequencies for each map unit (i.e., number of polygons) along with acreage per map unit are listed in Table 6.

Normally the standard minimum mapping unit for NPS vegetation mapping projects is defined as 0.5 hectare. However this is a nominal unit and due to the small size of FOLS and the resolution of the imagery it was reduced to ¼ acre. This size allowed for more detail in the mapping and allowed for better delineation of important stands of vegetation such as wetlands, weedy patches and riparian vegetation. This ability to recognize small patches of vegetation is reflected in the high number of polygons created (1,898) and the average size of the polygons for this project, ~8 acres (3 hectares).

Table 6. Total acreage and frequency of map units for FOLS.

Map Code	Map Unit Description	Fort Larned			Ruts Area			Total Project Area		
		Freq.	Acres	HA	Freq.	Acres	HA	Freq.	Acres	HA
F-CTBW	*Populus deltoides - Salix nigra* Forest	11	11	4	1	0.1	0.1	12	11	4
F-GASH	*Fraxinus pennsylvanica - Ulmus* spp. *- Celtis occidentalis* Forest	34	45	18	0	0	0	36	74	30
H-BIGB	*Andropogon gerardii - Sorghastrum nutans* Western Great Plains Herbaceous Vegetation	0	0	0	2	2	1	2	2	1
H-BUFO	*Buchloe dactyloides* Planted/Cultivated Herbaceous Vegetation	20	23	9	0	0	0	20	23	9
H-JOHN	*Sorghum halepense* Herbaceous Alliance	1	0.4	0.2	0	0	0	1	0.4	0.2
H-OFLD	Old Field Weedy Herbaceous Vegetation	13	31	13	5	4	1	27	49	20
H-PDOG	Prairie Dog Town Grassland Complex	0	0	0	2	34	14	2	35	14
H-REPR	*Andropogon gerardii - (Sorghastrum nutans)* Herbaceous Alliance	27	122	49	5	4	2	32	200	81
H-SMBR	*Bromus inermis* Semi-natural Herbaceous Alliance	35	138	56	2	0.1	0.1	51	170	69
H-SMRT	Hydrologically Disturbed Seasonal *Polygonum* spp. Vegetation	0	0	0	1	0.3	0.1	1	0.3	0.1
H-WTWG	*Pascopyrum smithii* Herbaceous Alliance	3	2	1	0	0	0	3	2	1
L-AGRI	Agricultural Business	0	0	0	0	0	0	6	2	1
L-FACL	Park Facilities	13	2	1	0	0	0	13	2	1
L-FILD	Planted / Cultivated	12	247	100	2	0.4	0	18	1268	513
L-ROAD	Transportation	1	24	10	1	1	0.4	2	40	16
L-STRM	Stream / River	4	15	6	0	0	0	3	21	9
Total Land-Use / Land Cover		30	288	117	3	1	1	43	1334	540
Total Natural Vegetation		145	372	151	18	44	18	188	564	228
Totals		**175**	**660**	**267**	**21**	**45**	**18**	**229**	**1898**	**769**

Accuracy Assessment

The 2006 accuracy assessment effort yielded 106 points that were distributed throughout both sites of FOLS; none were sampled in the environs due to access constraints. Due to GPS receiver and location issues, one point was removed from the final analysis. In addition to their use in the AA analysis many of the points were also used to update the classification and to revise the local descriptions. These data helped strengthen the classification for FOLS and added to the global perspective of the individual types.

Actual analysis of the AA points involved a point-by-point review in two stages. During stage one, an AA GIS point file was created from the AA point coordinates recorded in the field. These were then overlaid on the vegetation map and a comparison of the final AA field call versus the vegetation polygon label was conducted by CTI staff. Initial comparisons resulted in a preliminary error matrix that was sent to SOPN for review. The first binary assessment revealed an overall accuracy of 92% with 1 map class falling below the 80% standard. However SOPN felt that this class was important for management and the accuracy was low likely due to the small sample size. Based on their recommendations the vegetation GIS layer was accepted and the preliminary analysis was finalized (Table 7).

Examination of the final error matrix (Table 7) shows that areas of confusion were found between similar herbaceous types. For example the Smooth Brome Semi-Natural Herbaceous Alliance type was confused four times with the Planted Semi - Natural Restored Grassland Prairie type and the Old Field Weedy Herbaceous Vegetation type was confused two times with the Planted Semi - Natural Restored Grassland Prairie type. Confusion is likely a result of similar species occurring in all of the grassland types. Species overlap such as this makes it difficult to correctly classify polygons since depending on local variations in the polygons could be accurately classified into all three of the map units.

The confusion of error in the grassland types points to a larger, more general trend of the accuracy assessment dealing with the differences in scale and perspective. Viewing the vegetation from an overhead image affords the observer with a more comprehensive picture of how the vegetation lies on the landscape. However, when a researcher travels to this polygon they do not have this perspective and may concentrate on small inclusions or local variations that are not characteristic of the polygon as a whole. For example, sampling could have occurred on smooth brome pockets or in grassland openings in the woodland canopies effectively capturing this vegetation type instead of the larger more prevalent type that was mapped.

Table 7. Contingency table (error matrix) for vegetation mapping at FOLS.

Map Units	F-CTBW	F-GASH	H-BIGB	H-BUFO	H-PDOG	H-REPR	H-OFLD	H-SMBR	H-SMRT	Totals	Commission Accuracy	90% Conf. Interval −	90% Conf. Interval +
F-CTBW	6	0	0	0	0	0	0	0	0	6	100%	92%	100%
F-GASH	0	19	0	1	0	0	0	0	0	20	95%	84%	100%
H-BIGB	0	0	3	0	0	0	0	0	0	3	100%	83%	100%
H-BUFO	0	0	0	5	0	0	0	0	0	5	100%	90%	100%
H-PDOG	0	0	0	0	12	0	0	0	0	12	100%	96%	100%
H-REPR	0	0	0	0	1	29	0	0	0	30	97%	90%	100%
H-OFLD	0	0	0	0	0	2	5	0	0	7	71%	36%	100%
H-SMBR	0	0	0	0	0	4	0	17	0	21	81%	64%	97%
H-SMRT	0	0	0	0	0	0	0	0	1	1	100%	50%	100%
Totals	6	19	3	6	13	35	5	17	1				
Omission Accuracy	100%	100%	100%	83%	92%	81%	100%	100%	100%				
90% Conf. Level −	92%	97%	83%	50%	76%	68%	90%	97%	50%				
90% Conf. Level +	100%	100%	100%	100%	100%	93%	100%	100%	100%				

Producer' Error — Sample Data (Polygon Map Data); Reference Data (Accuracy Assessment Field Data); User's Error

Overall Total Accuracy = 92%   Overall Kappa Index = 89%   Overall 90% Upper and Lower Confidence Interval = 85% and 96%

97 Total Correct Points   105 Total Points

Please Note: One point was removed from the analysis since it occurred on a park special polygon that was previously documented with a plot.

<u>Instructions on Using the Accuracy Assessment Contingency Table:</u>

The contingency table or error matrix found above presents an array of numbers set out in rows and columns corresponding to a particular vegetation map unit relative to the actual vegetation type as verified on the ground. The column headings represent the vegetation classification as determined in the field and the row headings represent the vegetation classification taken from the vegetation map. The highlighted diagonal indicates the number of points assessed in the field that agree with the map label. Conversely, the inaccuracies of each map unit are described as both errors of inclusion (user's or commission errors) and errors of exclusion (producer's or omission errors). By reading across this table (i.e., rows) one can calculate the percent error of commission, or how many polygons for each map unit were incorrectly labeled when compared to the field data. By reading down the table (i.e., columns) one can calculate the percent error of omission, or how many polygons for that type were left off the map. Numbers "on the diagonal" tell the user how well the map unit was interpreted and how confident they can be in using it. Numbers "off the diagonal" yield important information about the deficiencies of the map including which types were: 1) over- mapped - commission errors on the right or 2) under-mapped - omission errors on the bottom

Discussion

Fort Larned National Historic Site is truly a special place combining an unique mix of historically important structures, agricultural lands, and remnants of native plant communities. Across this fragmented landscape a wide array of native and exotic plants thrive in habitats typical of the Southern Plains, including the Pawnee River Valley. The multiple uses on this landscape made it very challenging to both classify and map the vegetation into meaningful context for all levels of interest (local, regional and national). However, due to the small size of the park and the accessibility afforded for the sampling crews and verification efforts, a highly accurate classification and map was completed. Even though the accuracy is high there are still some areas were improvements can be made, which are summarized below.

Field Survey

The vegetation data presented in this project should be used as a "baseline" to build upon. New survey work in a timely manner would greatly improve both the classification and mapping efforts. Using the accuracy assessment as a guide, map classes with lower accuracy could be further surveyed in the field to create more accurate delineations. While it may appear that there are a large number of associations and alliances described for this small study area, some of the associations/alliances were either only minimally sampled or not sampled at all due to access constraints. It is recommended that these types should receive additional survey work to further define their classification. For example some of the herbaceous types should be examined throughout the growing year to document both the cool and warm season species in order to refine their composition. Also, accessing neighboring private lands would allow new plot samples to be obtained increasing the confidence in these types, thereby strengthening the classification.

NVC Classification

Along with access onto private lands the other main classification challenge at FOLS is keeping up with the rapid changes to plant life caused by agricultural manipulation and anthropogenic disturbance. Changes include tree removal, prairie restoration, wild fires, and flooding. At all times, but especially after these events, new data should be collected to reflect these changes. For example, as the park continues to restore its tallgrass prairie, this type may later need to be classified using a more natural association such as a Big Bluestem – Indiangrass community type. Overall more specialized and targeted data collection in these areas would help to document any changes and would greatly increase our understanding of these types in general.

Digital Imagery and Interpretation

The decision to purchase new CIR imagery for FOLS greatly aided the vegetation mapping process. In the future it may be beneficial to continue to work with KU and purchase new orthophotos or aerial photos exclusively for updating the vegetation map at FOLS. By continuing to purchase affordable imagery the park maintains better control over when the imagery is acquired. Thoughtful timing allows them to better match the imagery to the peak growing stage and insures that the imagery is cloud and shadow free. Although the NAIP imagery is free it is not acquired by the USDA for the purpose of vegetation mapping. For future mapping efforts the park should weigh the cost savings of this free imagery against the better detail afforded by custom CIR products. Also, due to the small size of the park, a finer scale of imagery (such as 1:6,000) or new digital cameras that capture both the visible and infrared bands could be used allowing for more precise delineations.

Inherent to all vegetation mapping projects is the need to produce both a consistent vegetation classification and a comprehensive set of map units. Typically the systems are very similar, but when using a national classification such as the NVC there is usually not a strict one-to-one correspondence. Nonconformity is due to the remote sensing nature of the interpretation and its ability to delineate map units based on complex photo signatures. Subtle vegetation characteristics that can be seen on the ground are not necessarily the same as those apparent on the imagery. Canopy closure, shadows, and the timing of the imagery acquisition can all impact the vegetation signatures. At FOLS these issues can be offset not only by acquiring new imagery but also by conducting more map verification or ground-truthing. Increasing the amount of time and money budgeted for verification of the map would greatly improve the accuracy and level of detail. Similarly, this work should only be viewed as an initial mapping effort that needs to be refined and periodically updated. To perform field checking, the existing map could be examined in the field by qualified park or contract staff, changes could be made to the map and these could be incorporated into new versions that would keep the product current over the years.

Accuracy Assessment

An important and necessary aspect of this project is the accuracy assessment. Collecting independent ground data determines the usefulness of the vegetation map. As such, users of this product should remember that the GIS mapping and classification portions of the project were conducted separately from both the plot and AA field data collection. These three divisions in work created some challenges related to communication among all the teams, including: (1) adequately conveying changes to the classification based on revising the preliminary associations as recorded in the field into the NVC, (2) mapping some types less than the one-quarter acre minimum mapping unit, (3) mapping new associations/alliances found in the environs but not found in the park, and (4) generally providing enough instruction and interaction to the field crews to explain how these changes would effect the AA.

Specifically at FOLS, new associations and alliances occurring either as very small sites in the park or occurring in the environs should have been marked as such in the field key. Field key notes would have indicated to the crews that they would probably not encounter some types in the AA and if they did, these associations would be new and should be sampled with a full plot and not an AA point. Also it should have been explained or documented which preliminary associations corresponded to the newly classified NVC associations. For example, CTI added the Western Wheatgrass Herbaceous Alliance and Johnsongrass Herbaceous Alliance types to the classification. These were not sampled by KSNHI which may have led to some confusion when the field team accessed sites that only contained western wheatgrass or Johnsongrass.

Finally insufficient interaction between the field and GIS teams created some scale-related issues. As mentioned previously, looking at vegetation from an overhead perspective varies greatly from seeing it on the ground. Because of the extensive field exposure to the vegetation at FOLS, the field team was very knowledgeable about the parks' habitats. Onsite knowledge included a thorough understanding of when one association changed to another either due to succession or due to an ecotone. Since the mapping team was tasked to provide a map of the existing vegetation the delineation on the map did not always match what the field team viewed as the break between plant associations. Similarly small stands of vegetation that were accurately mapped on the aerial photography were seen by the field crews as actually being inclusions in larger units and vice versa. This discrepancy could also be defined as stemming from the fundamental difference between deriving vegetation from imagery signatures versus ecological or field experience. In the future it would be helpful if more communication could occur between all teams involved. This communication would at a minimum include multiple field visits by all teams at the same time.

Future Recommendations

In summary, this project represents the best efforts put forth by a multi-disciplined team over a relatively short period in time. In order to create the best possible "long-term" vegetation classification for FOLS and the most accurate and detailed GIS layer, this project should be viewed as a place to start rather than an end product. In other words, present and future NPS staff should be encouraged to scrutinize this project, building from its strengths and bolstering its weaknesses. By keeping in mind that this project was only a snapshot in time, future efforts can help complete our understanding of the vegetation in and around FOLS and how it changes. It is the hope of the producers that the products presented here will help focus and direct future efforts. The following recommendations are summarized below.

1. The diversity of plant species and dynamic nature of the park with respect to the agricultural aspect warrants periodic **field surveys** by experienced ecologists. Further the inaccessibility of the private lands in the environs should be addressed by seeking permission to sample and verify the vegetation. In this way new plant associations could be discovered and existing types could be updated.

2. Remote sensing does not replace on-the-ground knowledge provided by GPS-linked plots, observations and ground verification. Time and funding limitations curtailed the amount of map **ground-truthing** performed. As opportunities arise, maps should be examined in the field by experienced crews. Also GPS receiver data and other GIS layers should be used to improve and update the spatial data. This map product should not be viewed as static but should be updated with more current and accurate information.

3. To better understand the limitations of the map, the **accuracy assessment** data presented in Table 7 should be thoroughly reviewed by the park staff. Map classes with low accuracy should be examined to see if they could be improved with future studies using ground-truthing or other remote-sensing formats (i.e. fine-scale imagery, hyperspectral, etc). Also, landscape modeling may help to tease out the location of specific types based on specific habitat information. Finally for some applications it may make sense to combine map classes into higher units, such as alliances or ecological systems to improve their accuracy.

4. For monitoring purposes, **change over time** could be addressed by similar remote sensing projects. New aerial photos or NAIP imagery acquired every year could be used in regular intervals to capture change. Specifically this new imagery could be used to create up-to-date vegetation layers that could be used to compare changes in both individual vegetation stands and across the entire park.

5. In the future, resource management personnel could link the habitat for **species of concern** to specific associations and map units. These map units could then be used to help locate potential sites of endangered or threatened species in the field or identify areas for non-native plant removal or treatment.

Research Opportunities

Having an accurate and current vegetation classification and map presents many new and exciting research opportunities. Research could include expanding or linking the GIS layer to derive other information such as fire models, habitat monitoring locations, guides for rare plant surveys, and inventorying areas that likely contain exotic or invasive species. The map could also be enhanced by overlaying other existing GIS layers such as geology, hydrology, elevation, and soils. In this manner complex interactions between these layers could be examined and yield important information about growth rates, regeneration after disturbance, biomass distribution, and stream morphology. Finally, through innovative analyses the vegetation layer could possibly be used as a springboard for other ecological studies such as examining how the vegetation interacts with soil chemistry, pollution, archeological sites, weather patterns, etc.

Literature Cited

Anderson, J.R., E.E. Hardy, J.T. Roach, R.E. Witmer. 1976. A land use and land cover classification system for use with remote sensor data. *Geological Survey Professional Paper 964.* Washington, DC: U.S. Government Printing Office.

Cowardin, L. M., V. Carter, F. C. Golet, and E. T. LaRoe. 1979. Classification of wetlands and deepwater habitats of the United States. U.S. Fish and Wildlife Service, Biological Service Program. FWS/OBS-79/31. Washington, DC. 103 pp.

Daubenmire, R. 1959. A canopy-coverage method of vegetational analysis. Northwest Science. 23: 69-82.

Federal Geographic Data Committee Vegetation Subcomittee. 1997. Vegetation Classification Standard. June 1997. FGDC-STD-005.
Available: http://biology.usgs.gov/fgdc.veg/standards/vegstd.

Great Plains Flora Association. 1986. Flora of the Great Plains. Lawrence, Kansas, University Press of Kansas.

Grossman D.H., D. Faber-Langendoen, A.S. Weakley, M. Anderson, P. Bourgeron, R. Crawford, K. Goodin, S. Landaal, K. Metzler, K.D. Patterson, M. Pyne, M. Reid, and L. Sneddon. 1998. International classification of ecological communities: terrestrial vegetation of the United States. Volume I, The National Vegetation Classification System: development, status, and applications. The Nature Conservancy: Arlington, VA.
Available: http://www.natureserve.org/publications/library.jsp#nspubs.

Grossman, D.H., K.L. Goodin, X. Li, D. Faber-Langendoen, M. Anderson, and R. Vaughan, Establishing standards for field methods and mapping procedures. 1994. Prepared for the USGS-NPS Vegetation Mapping Program by The Nature Conservancy, Arlington VA, and Environmental Science Research Institute, Redlands, CA.

Hansen, Monica, J. Coles, K. Thomas, D. Cogan, M. Ried, J. VonLoh, and K. Schulz. 2004. USGS-NPS National Vegetation Mapping Program: Wupatki National Monument, Arizona, Vegetation Classification and Distribution. Final Report. U.S. Geological Survey Southwest Biological Science Center. Flagstaff, AZ.

Lauver, C.L., K. Kindscher, D. Faber-Langendoen, and R. Schneider. 1999. A classification of the natural vegetation of Kansas. The Southwestern Naturalist 44:421-443.

NatureServe. 2006. NatureServe Explorer: An online encyclopedia of life [web application]. Version 4.7. NatureServe, Arlington, Virginia. Available http://www.natureserve.org/explorer. (Accessed: May 24, 2006).

Salas, D., J. Stevens, K. Schulz. 2004. USGS-NPS National Vegetation Mapping Program: Rocky Mountain National Park. Final Report. U.S. Bureau of Reclamation Remote Sensing and GIS Group Technical Memorandum 8260-05-02. Denver, Colorado.

The Nature Conservancy and Environmental Research Systems Institute. 1994a. NBS/NPS Vegetation Mapping Program: Standardized National Vegetation Classification System. Arlington, VA.

The Nature Conservancy and Environmental Research Systems Institute. 1994b. NBS/NPS Vegetation Mapping Program: Field Methods for Vegetation Mapping. Arlington,

The Nature Conservancy and Environmental Research Systems Institute. 1994c. *NBS/NPS Vegetation Mapping Program: Accuracy Assessment Procedures.* Arlington, VA.

The Nature Conservancy. 1997. PLOTS Database System, Version 1.1. The Nature Conservancy, Arlington, VA.

APPENDIX A: Components and Flow Diagram of the Vegetation Classification and Mapping Program

(Developed by Tom Owens USGS – BRD)

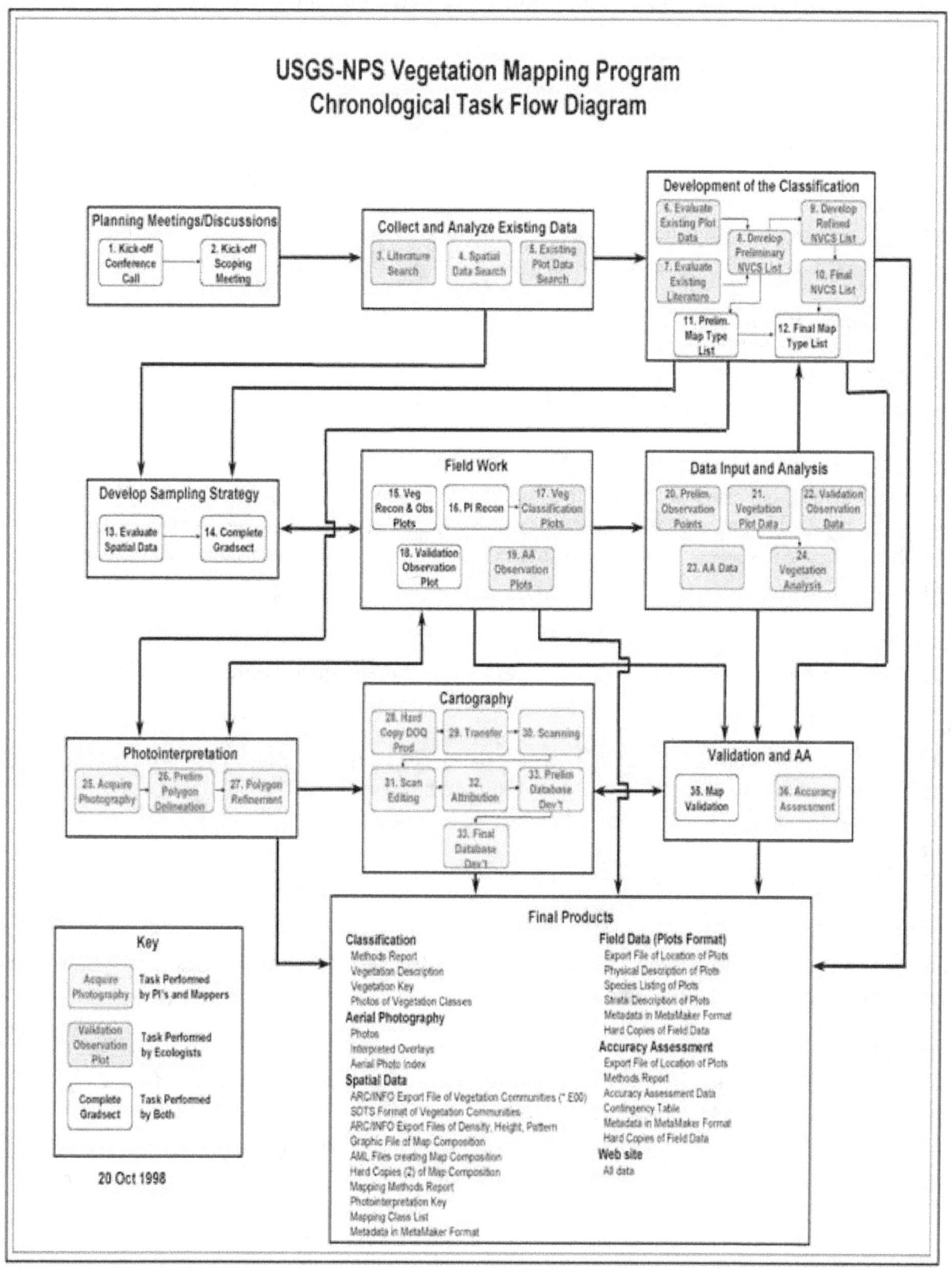

APPENDIX B: Field Data Forms and Instructions

General instructions for filling out fields
in the PLOT SURVEY FORM (adapted from Salas et al. 2004)

IDENTIFIERS/LOCATORS

Plot Code
Code indicating the specific plot within the vegetation polygon.

Surveyors
Names of surveyors, with principal surveyor listed first.

Date
Date the survey was taken; year, month, day.

BPU Code
The biophysical unit identified.

Provisional Community Name
Using the provisional classification of the Park that was provided, assign the name of the vegetation type which most closely resembles this type. Enter the finest level of the classification possible. If it's a new type, name it based on the two or three most dominant species in the plot.

Quad Name
Appropriate name/scale from survey map used; use 7.5-minute quadrangle if possible.

Park Site Name
Provisional name assigned by field worker that describes where the data were collected. It should represent an identifiable feature on a topographic map.

GPS Rover File
Record the number of the file from the GPS unit.

Field UTM X
Use GPS; do not estimate. If you can't get a GPS reading, estimate coordinates from a topo map and note on the form that this method was used.

Field UTM Y
Use GPS; do not estimate. If you can't get a GPS reading, estimate coordinates from a topo map and note on the form that this method was used.

Error
Record this off the GPS unit.

Plot Length and Plot Width
Enter width and length dimensions for square or rectangular plots. Choose the appropriate plot size based on the following:

Vegetation Class	Standard Plot Dimensions	PLOT AREA
Forest	20 m x 20 m	400 m^2
Woodland	20 m x 20 m	400 m^2
Shrubland	20 m x 20 m	400 m^2
Dwarf-shrubland (heath)	10 m x 10 m	100 m^2
Herbaceous	10 m x 10 m	100 m^2
Nonvascular	5 m x 5 m	25 m^2

Photo numbers
If photos of the plot have been taken at the time of sampling, indicate their numbers from the ones the camera assigns.

Plot Permanent
Note if the plot has been permanently marked.

Plot Representativeness
Does this plot represent the full variability of the polygon? If not, were additional plots taken? Note: we distinguish in this section the plot's ability to represent the stand or polygon you are sampling as one component, and the ability of this sample to represent the range of variability of the association in the entire mapping area. The former comment may be ascertained by reconnaissance of the stand. The latter comment comes only after some familiarity with the vegetation type throughout the mapping area and may be left blank if you have no opinion at this time.

ENVIRONMENTAL DESCRIPTION

Elevation
Elevation of the plot obtained from the GPS

Slope
Measure the slope in percent using a clinometer.

Aspect
Measure the aspect using a compass (be sure compass is set to correct for the magnetic declination).

Topographic Position
Choose one:

> INTERFLUVE (crest, summit, ridge). Linear top of ridge, hill, or mountain; the elevated area between two fluves (drainageways) that sheds water to the drainageways.

> SHOULDER (shoulder slope, upper slope, convex creep slope). Geomorphic component that forms the uppermost inclined surface at the top of a slope. Includes the transition zone from backslope to summit. Surface is dominantly convex in profile and erosional in origin.

> BACKSLOPE. Subset of midslopes that are steep, linear, and may include cliff segments (fall faces).

> FOOTSLOPE (lower slope, foot slope, colluvial footslope). Inner gently inclined surface at the base of a slope. Surface profile is generally concave and a transition between backslope, and toeslope.

> TOESLOPE (alluvial toeslope). Outermost gently inclined surface at base of a slope. In profile, commonly gentle and linear and characterized by alluvial deposition.

> TERRACE Valley floor or shoreline representing the former position of an alluvial plain, lake, or shore.

> CHANNEL (narrow valley bottom, gully arroyo). Bed of single or braided watercourse commonly barren of vegetation and formed of modern alluvium.

> BASIN FLOOR (depression). Nearly level to gently sloping, bottom surface of a basin.

Describe Topographic Position (Optional)
Give more details here, if needed.

Cowardin System
Indicate "upland" if the system is not a wetland. If the system is a wetland, check off the name of the USFWS system which best describes its hydrology and landform.

- Riverine: Below the high water mark on a moving water system (a creek bed). A community of *Eleocharis* on a sand bar would be in this category.
- Palustrine: In the riparian zone. Plants regularly have wet roots through much of the summer. A community of willows and sedges would be in this category.
- Lacustrine: Below the high water mark of a lake. The marshy stuff on the edge of a lake would be in this category.

Assess the hydrologic regime of the plot using the descriptions below (adapted from Cowardin et al. 1979).

PERMANENTLY FLOODED - Water covers the land surface at all times of the year in all years. Equivalent to Cowardin's "permanently flooded."

SEMIPERMANENTLY FLOODED - Surface water persists throughout growing season in most years except during periods of drought. Land surface is normally saturated when water level drops below soil surface. Includes Cowardin's Intermittently Exposed and Semipermanently Flooded modifiers.

SEASONALLY FLOODED - Surface water is present for extended periods during the growing season, but is absent by the end of the growing season in most years. The water table after flooding ceases is very variable, extending from saturated to a water table well below the ground surface. Includes Cowardin's Seasonal, Seasonal-Saturated, and Seasonal-Well Drained modifiers.

SATURATED - Surface water is seldom present, but substrate is saturated to surface for extended periods during the growing season. Equivalent to Cowardin's Saturated modifier.

TEMPORARILY FLOODED - Surface water present for brief periods during growing season, but water table usually lies well below soil surface. Often characterizes flood-plain wetlands. Equivalent to Cowardin's Temporary modifier.

INTERMITTENTLY FLOODED - Substrate is usually exposed, but surface water can be present for variable periods without detectable seasonal periodicity. Inundation is not predictable to a given season and is dependent upon highly localized rain storms. This modifier was developed for use in the arid West for water regimes of Playa lakes, intermittent streams, and dry washes but can be used in other parts of the U.S. where appropriate. This modifier can be applied to both wetland and non-wetland situations. Equivalent to Cowardin's Intermittently Flooded modifier.

UNKNOWN - The water regime of the area is not known. The unit is simply described as a non-tidal wetland.

Unvegetated Surface
Estimate the approximate percentage of the *total* surface area covered by each category.

Soil Texture
Using the key below, assess average soil texture.

Simplified Key to Soil Texture
Soil does not remain in a ball when squeezed...sand
Soil remains in a ball when squeezed..2

Squeeze the ball between your thumb and forefinger, attempting to make a ribbon that you can push up over your finger.
    2.   Soil makes no ribbon...loamy sand
    2.   Soil makes a ribbon (may be very short)...3

    3. Ribbon extends less than 1 inch before breaking...4
Add excess water to small amount of soil:

        4. Soil feels smooth...silt loam
        4. Soil feels at least slightly gritty...5
Squeeze a moistened ball:
5. Cast is formed which can be handled CAREFULLY without breaking........... sandy loam
5. Cast is formed which can be handled FREELY without breaking...... ....loam

    3. Ribbon extends 1 inch or more before breaking..6

        5. Soil makes a ribbon that breaks when 1 to 2 inches long; cracks if bent into a ring...7

Add excess water to small amount of soil:
        7. Soil feels at least slightly gritty..clay loam
        7. Soil feels smooth...silt

      6. Soil makes a ribbon 2+ inches long; does NOT crack when bent into a ring............ 8
Add excess water to a small amount of soil:

        8. Soil feels at least slightly gritty..............................clay
        8. Soil feels smooth..silty clay

HANDBOOK ON SOILS

In the field, soil texture is determined by the feel of a moist soil when it is rubbed between the thumb and fingers. Since sand particles feel gritty, silt particles have a smooth velvety feel and clay is both sticky and plastic, an estimate of the relative proportions of the separates may be made. This procedure, of course, will not give the exact percentage of sand, silt, and clay, but, with a little practice on samples of known composition, the relative proportions of the individual separates can be closely estimated. Practice with known samples is the only way to acquire this knowledge.

The outstanding physical characteristics of the main textural grades as determined by the feel of the soil are described below.

1. Sandy Soil. A sandy soil is loose and single grained. The individual grains can be seen readily or felt. Squeezed in the hand when dry, it will fall apart when pressure is released. Squeezed when moist, it will form a cast, but will crumble when touched.

2. Sandy Loam Soil. A sandy loam soil contains much sand, but has enough silt and clay to make it somewhat coherent. Individual sand grains can be easily seen and felt. Squeezed when dry, it will form a cast which will readily fall apart; but if squeezed when moist a cast can be formed which will bear careful handling without breaking.

3. Loam Soil. A loam soil is about an equal mixture of the sand and silt with the clay content being between 7 and 27 percent. A loam is mellow with a somewhat sandy feel, yet fairly smooth and slightly plastic. Squeezed when moist, it will form a cast which can be handled freely without breaking.

4. Silt Loam Soil. A silt loam soil, when dry, may appear cloddy, but lumps are readily broken, and when pulverized, it feels soft and floury. When wet, the soil readily runs together. Either dry or moist, it will form casts which can be handled freely without breaking, but when moistened and extruded between the thumb and fingers, it will not form a ribbon, but will give a broken appearance.

5. Clay Loam Soil. A clay loam soil is fine-textured and usually breaks into clods or lumps that are hard when dry. When moist and extruded between the thumb and fingers, it will form a thin "ribbon" which will break readily, barely sustaining its own weight. The moist soil is plastic and will form a cast that will bear much handling. When kneaded in the hand, it does not crumble readily, but tends to work into a heavy, compact mass.

6. Clay Soil. A clay soil is fine-textured and usually forms very hard lumps or clods when dry and is plastic and sticky when wet. When the moist soil is ribboned out between the thumb and fingers, it will form a long flexible strip. A clay soil leaves a "slick' surface on the thumb and fingers when rubbed together and tends to hold the thumb and fingers together due to the stickiness of the clay.

The characteristics described above are suggestive only, and will only apply to a group of similar soils. The characteristics of clay vary with the kind of clay mineral. For this reason, textural grades may exhibit different properties from region to region. For instance, clays of the montmorillonite group are very sticky and plastic; those of the oxide group are plastic and waxy with relatively little stickiness.

The preceding discussion has been directed to those soil particles whose diameters are less than 2 millimeters--the sands, silts, and clays. Soils may also contain larger sized particles that may be collectively called coarse fragments. These large particles may on occasion exceed the smaller soil particles in volume.

Soil Drainage

The soil drainage classes are defined in terms of (1) actual moisture content (in excess of field moisture capacity) and (2) the extent of the period during which excess water is present in the plant-root zone. It is recognized that permeability, level of groundwater, and seepage are factors affecting moisture status. However, because these are not easily observed or measured in the field, they cannot generally be used as criteria of moisture status. It is further recognized that soil profile morphology, for example mottling, normally, but not always, reflects soil moisture status. Although soil morphology may be a valuable field indication of moisture status, it should not be the overriding criterion. Soil drainage classes cannot be based solely on the presence or absence of mottling. Topographic position and vegetation as well as soil morphology are useful field criteria for assessing soil moisture status.

> WELL DRAINED - The soil moisture content does not normally exceed field capacity in any horizon (except possibly the C) for a significant part of the year.

> MODERATELY WELL DRAINED - The soil moisture content is in excess of field capacity for a small but significant period of the year.

> POORLY DRAINED - The soil moisture content is in excess of field capacity in all horizons for a large part of the year.

VEGETATION DESCRIPTION

Leaf Phenology
Select the value which best describes the leaf phenology of the dominant stratum. The dominant stratum is the uppermost stratum that contains at least 10% cover.

> EVERGREEN - Greater than 75% of the total woody cover is never without green foliage.

> COLD DECIDUOUS - Greater than 75% of the total woody cover sheds its foliage in connection with an unfavorable season mainly characterized by winter frost.

MIXED: EVERGREEN & COLD DECIDUOUS - Evergreen and deciduous species generally contribute 25-75% of the total woody cover. Evergreen and cold-deciduous species are mixed.

PERENNIAL - Herbaceous vegetation composed of more than 50% perennial species.

ANNUAL - Herbaceous vegetation composed of more than 50% annual species.

Leaf Type
Select the value which best describes the leaf form of the dominant stratum. The dominant stratum is the uppermost stratum that contains at least 10% cover.

BROAD-LEAVED - Woody vegetation primarily broad-leaved (generally contributes greater than 50 percent of the total woody cover).

NEEDLE-LEAVED - Woody vegetation primarily needle-leaved (generally contributes greater than 50 percent cover).

GRAMINOID - Herbaceous vegetation composed of more than 50 percent graminoid/stipe leaf species.

FORB (BROAD-LEAF-HERBACEOUS) - Herbaceous vegetation composed of more than 50% broad-leaf forb species.

PTERIDOPHYTE - Herbaceous vegetation composed of more than 50 percent species with frond or frond-like leaves. (Ferns)

Physiognomic Class
Choose one:
Forest: Trees with their crowns overlapping (generally forming 60-100% cover).

Woodland: Open stands of trees with crowns not usually touching (generally forming 25-60% cover). Canopy tree cover may be less than 25% in cases where it exceeds shrub, dwarf-shrub, herb, and nonvascular cover.

Shrubland: Shrubs generally greater than 2.5 feet tall with individuals or clumps overlapping to not touching (generally forming more than 25% cover, trees generally less than 25% cover). Shrub cover may be less than 25% where it exceeds tree, dwarf-shrub, herb, and nonvascular cover.

Dwarf-Shrubland: Low-growing shrubs usually under 2.5 feet tall. Individuals or clumps overlapping to not touching (generally forming more than 25% cover, trees and tall shrubs generally less than 25% cover). Dwarf-shrub cover may be less than 25% where it exceeds tree, shrub, herb, and nonvascular cover.

Herbaceous: Herbs (graminoids, forbs, and ferns) dominant (generally forming at least 25% cover; trees, shrubs, and dwarf-shrubs generally with less than 25% cover). Herb cover may be less than 25% where it exceeds tree, shrub, dwarf-shrub, and nonvascular cover.

Nonvascular: Nonvascular cover (bryophytes, non-crustose lichens, and algae) dominant (generally forming at least 25% cover). Nonvascular cover may be less than 25% where it exceeds tree, shrub, dwarf-shrub, and herb cover.

Sparse Vegetation: Abiotic substrate features dominant. Vegetation is scattered to nearly absent and generally restricted to areas of concentrated resources (total vegetation cover is typically less than 25% and greater than 0%).

Strata, Height Class, Cover Class, Diagnostic Species
Visually divide the community into vegetation layers (strata). Indicate the average height class of the stratum in the first column, using the Height Scale on the form. Enter the average percent cover class of the whole stratum in the second column, using the Cover Scale on the form. Height and Cover classes are also listed below.

Trees are defined as single-stemmed woody plants, generally 15 feet in height or greater at maturity and under optimal growing conditions. Shrubs are defined as multiple-stemmed woody plants generally less than 15 feet in height at maturity and under optimal growing conditions.

List the dominant species in each stratum.

Animal Use Evidence
Comment on any evidence of wildlife (i.e., tracks, scat, gopher or prairie dog mounds, etc.). Notes on domestic animals should be made in the field below.

Natural and Anthropogenic Disturbance
Comment on any evidence of natural or anthropogenic disturbance and specify the source.

Environmental Comments
Enter any additional noteworthy comments on the environmental setting. This field can be used to describe site history such as fire events (date since last fire or evidence of severity) as well as other disturbance or reproduction factors

Other Comments
Any miscellaneous comments.

Species/Strata/Percent Cover Table

The main use of the strata information is to categorize the plots by life form, in order to subset the data into forest, woodland, shrublands, and herbaceous plots for analysis. It is imperative that things be called the same throughout the data set.

Starting with the uppermost stratum, list all the species present and their cover class using the scale provided below. If a species is in the tree layer (single-stemmed woody plants, generally 15 feet in height or greater at maturity), list whether it is T1 (emergent tree), T2 (tree canopy), or T3 (tree sub-canopy). If a species is in the shrub layer, note if S1 (tall shrub), or S2 (short shrub), or S3 (dwarf shrub). If in the ground layer, note if H (herbaceous), N (nonvascular). Some species will be in more than one layer. For example, Cottonwoods might have one or two especially tall specimens, which would be in the T1 (emergent tree) layer. Then the majority of the mature trees would be in T2 (tree canopy). The saplings that are coming up in the understory would be in the T3.

Seedlings are defined as trees less than "breast height" or less than 4.5 feet tall. Seedlings between knee height and breast height should be labeled as being in the short shrub layer (S2), and those below knee height should be labeled as being in the dwarf shrub layer (S3).

Cover Scale for Species Percent Cover

Use the cover scales provided on the forms.

NATIONAL PARK VEGETATION MAPPING PROGRAM: PLOT SURVEY FORM

IDENTIFIERS/LOCATORS

Plot Code_____ Polygon Code_____

Provisional Community Name_____

State ____ Park Name_____ Park Site Name_____

Quad Name_____ Quad Code_____

GPS file name_____ Field UTM X __ __ __ __ __ m E Field UTM Y __ __ __ __ __ __ __ m N

Error +/-_____ m

please do not complete the following information when in the field
Corrected UTM X __ __ __ __ __ __ m E Corrected UTM Y __ __ __ __ __ __ __ m N   UTM Zone_____

Survey Date_____ Surveyors_____

Directions to Plot

Plot length_____ Plot width_____ Plot Photos (y/n) ___ Roll Number _____ Frame Number _____ Plot Permanent (y/n) ____

Plot representativeness

ENVIRONMENTAL DESCRIPTION

| Elevation _____ Slope _____ Aspect_____ |
| Topographic Position |
| Landform |
| Surficial Geology |

| Cowardian System
___ Upland
___ Riverine
___ Palustrine
___ Lacustrine | Non-Tidal
___ Permanently Flooded
___ Semipermanetly Flooded
___ Seasonally/Temporarily Flooded | ___ Saturated
___ Seasonally Flooded/Saturated
___ Intermittently Flooded | |

Environmental Comments:	Soil Taxon/Description
	Unvegetated Surface: *(please use the cover scale on next page)* ___ Bedrock ___ Litter, duff ___ Wood (> 1 cm) ___ Large rocks (cobbles, boulders > 10 cm) ___ Small rocks (gravel, 0.2-10 cm) ___ Sand (0.1-2 mm) ___ Bare soil ___ Other:_____
Soil Texture ___ sand ___ loamy sand ___ sandy loam ___ loam ___ silt loam ___ silt ___ clay loam ___ silty clay ___ clay ___ peat ___ muck	Soil Drainage ___ Rapidly drained ___ Well drained ___ Moderately well drained ___ Somewhat poorly drained ___ Poorly drained ___ Very poorly drained

VEGETATION DESCRIPTION

Leaf phenology (of dominant stratum)	Leaf Type (of dominant stratum)	Physiognomic class	Cover Scale for Strata & Unvegetated Surface		Height Scale for Strata	
		___ Forest				
Trees and Shrubs	___ Broad-leaved	___ Woodland	01	5%	01	<0.5 m
___ Evergreen	___ Needle-leaved	___ Shrubland	02	10%	02	0.5-1m
___ Cold-deciduous	___ Microphyllous	___ Dwarf Shrubland	03	20%	03	1-2 m
___ Drought-deciduous	___ Graminoid	___ Herbaceous	04	30%	04	2-5 m
___ Mixed evergreen - cold-deciduous	___ Forb	___ Nonvascular	05	40%	05	5-10 m
___ Mixed evergreen - drought-deciduous	___ Pteridophyte	___ Sparsely Vegetated	06	50%	06	10-15 m
			07	60%	07	15-20 m
Herbs			08	70%	08	20-35 m
___ Annual			09	80%	09	35 - 50 m
___ Perennial			10	90%	10	>50 m
			11	100%		

Strata	Height Class	Cover Class	Diagnostic species (if known)
T1 Emergent			_____
T2 Canopy			_____
T3 Sub-canopy			_____
S1 Tall shrub			_____
S2 Short Shrub			_____
H Herbaceous			_____
N Non-vascular			_____
V Vine-liana			_____
E Epiphyte			_____

please see above table for height and cover scales

Animal Use Evidence

Natural and Anthropogenic Disturbance Comments

Other Comments

Plot Code

Species/percent cover: Starting with the uppermost stratum, list all species with % cover for each species in the stratum. For each tree species estimate seedling, sapling, mature and total cover indicating stratum. Also for forests and woodlands, on a separate page or line below each tree species, list the DBH of all trees above 5 cm diameter. Separate measurements with a comma (note if measurements are from multi-stemmed tree). Put an asterisk next to any species that are known diagnostics for a particular community in the classification. **Also list species outside the plot at the end of the table or designate with a 0 in Cover Class column.**

Stratum	Species Name	Cover Class	Stratum	Species Name	Cover Class	Stratum	Species Name	Cover Class

```
Cover Class Scale
T = >0-1%      5 = >45-55%
P = >1-5%      6 = >55-65%
1 = >5-15%     7 = >65-75%
2 = >15-25%    8 = >75-85%
3 = >25-35%    9 = >85-95%
4 = >35-45%    10 = >95%
```

Tree D.B.H Form
Plot Code:_____Units in cm or inches (circle one)
Record tree diameter over 5 cm at 4.5 feet (1.37 m) height for species that contribute to tree canopy.
Separate measurements of multi-stemmed trees with commas. Can estimate by 5 cm dia. classes

Species	D.B.H.(s) for multi-stems trees	Species	D.B.H.(s) for multi-stems trees
_____	_____	_____	_____
_____	_____	_____	_____
_____	_____	_____	_____
_____	_____	_____	_____
_____	_____	_____	_____
_____	_____	_____	_____
_____	_____	_____	_____
_____	_____	_____	_____
_____	_____	_____	_____
_____	_____	_____	_____
_____	_____	_____	_____
_____	_____	_____	_____
_____	_____	_____	_____
_____	_____	_____	_____
_____	_____	_____	_____
_____	_____	_____	_____
_____	_____	_____	_____
_____	_____	_____	_____
_____	_____	_____	_____
_____	_____	_____	_____
_____	_____	_____	_____
_____	_____	_____	_____
_____	_____	_____	_____
_____	_____	_____	_____
_____	_____	_____	_____
_____	_____	_____	_____
_____	_____	_____	_____
_____	_____	_____	_____
_____	_____	_____	_____
_____	_____	_____	_____
_____	_____	_____	_____
_____	_____	_____	_____
_____	_____	_____	_____
_____	_____	_____	_____
_____	_____	_____	_____
_____	_____	_____	_____
_____	_____	_____	_____
_____	_____	_____	_____
_____	_____	_____	_____
_____	_____	_____	_____
_____	_____	_____	_____
_____	_____	_____	_____

NATIONAL PARK VEGETATION MAPPING PROGRAM: OBSERVATION POINT FORM (1997)

IDENTIFIERS/LOCATORS

Plot Code_____ Polygon Code_____
Provisional Community Name_____
State ____ Park Name _____ Park Site Name _____
Quad Name_____ Quad Code_____
GPS file name_____ Field UTM X___ ___ ___ ___ ___ ___ m E Field UTM Y___ ___ ___ ___ ___ ___ ___ m N
please do not complete the following information when in the field Corrected UTM X___ ___ ___ ___ ___ ___ m E Corrected UTM Y___ ___ ___ ___ ___ ___ ___ m N   UTM Zone_____
Survey Date_____ Surveyors_____

ENVIRONMENTAL DESCRIPTION

Elevation _____ Slope _____ Aspect_____
Topographic Position
Landform

Cowardian System	Hydrologic Regime		Salinity Modifiers
___Upload	Non-Tidal		___Saltwater
___Riverine	___Permanently Flooded	___Saturated	___Brackish
___Palustrine	___Semipermanetly Flooded	___Temporarily Flooded/Saturated	___Freshwater
___Lacustrine	___Seasonally Flooded	___Intermittently Flooded	

Environmental Comments:	Unvegetated Surface: (please use the cover scale below)
	___ Bedrock ___ Litter, duff ___ Wood (> 1 cm)
	___ Large rocks (cobbles, boulders > 10 cm)
	___ Small rocks (gravel, 0.2-10 cm)
	___ Sand (0.1-2 mm) ___ Bare soil
	___ Other:_____

VEGETATION DESCRIPTION

Leaf phenology (of dominant stratum)	Leaf Type (of dominant stratum)	Physiognomic class	Cover Scale for Strata & Unvegetated Surface		Height Scale for Strata	
Trees and Shrubs ___Evergreen ___Cold-deciduous ___Drought-deciduous ___Mixed evergreen - cold-deciduous ___Mixed evergreen - drought-deciduous Herbs ___Annual ___Perennial	___Broad-leaved ___Needle-leaved ___Mixed broad-leaved/Needle leaved ___Microphyllous ___Graminoid ___Forb ___Pteridophyte	___Forest ___Woodland ___Shrubland ___Dwarf Shrubland ___Herbaceous ___Nonvascular ___Sparsely Vegetated	01 02 03 04 05 06 07 08 09 10 11	5% 10% 20% 30% 40% 50% 60% 70% 80% 90% 100%	01 02 03 04 05 06 07 08 09 10	<0.5 m 0.5-1m 1-2 m 2-5 m 5-10 m 10-15 m 15-20 m 20-35 m 35 - 50 m >50 m

Strata	Height	Cover Class	Dominant species (mark any known diagnostic species with a *)	Cover Class
T1 Emergent	_____	_____	_____	
			_____	
			_____	
T2 Canopy	_____	_____	_____	
			_____	
			_____	
			_____	
T3 Sub-canopy	_____	_____	_____	
			_____	
			_____	
S1 Tall shrub	_____	_____	_____	
			_____	
			_____	
			_____	
			_____	
S2 Short Shrub	_____	_____	_____	
			_____	
			_____	
			_____	
			_____	
S3 Dwarf-shrub	_____	_____	_____	
H Herbaceous			_____	
			_____	
			_____	
N Non-vascular	_____	_____	_____	
V Vine/liana	_____	_____	_____	
E Epiphyte	_____	_____	_____	

please see the table on the previous page for height and cover scales for strata

Other Comments	Cover Scale for Species
	01 <1%
	02 1-5%
	03 5-25%
	04 25-50%
	05 50-75%
	06 75-100%

FOLS Accuracy Assessment Form USGS-NPS Vegetation Mapping Program

1. *Plot (waypoint) Number* _____ 2. *Park Code*_____ *Date* _____

3. Observer(determined association) _____ 5. Observer (assisting) _____

6. GPS Unit make and model_____

7. GPS mode (circle all that apply)
    2D   3D-WAAS-enabled   3D-WAAS- disabled   Other (list)

8. Accuracy of Navigation (meters) _____ 9. How Determined _____

10. *UTM Easting* _____ 11. *UTM Northing* _____

12. UTM Zone _____   13.   Datum _____

14. Offset from Waypoint (if applicable) _____ meters _____ degrees bearing

15. Vegetation Association dominating Plot _____

16. Other possibility for dominant Association (as a complex) (if applicable) _____
_____

17. 2nd Association present (as a mosaic) in plot (if applicable) _____

18. 3rd Association present (as a mosaic) in plot (if applicable) _____

19. Dominant/characteristic species in tree layer (~ 1 – 5 species) _____
_____

20. Dominant/characteristic species in shrub layer (~ 1 – 5 species) _____
_____

21. Dominant/characteristic species in herbaceous layer (up to 10 species) _____
_____

22. Rationale for choice of dominant association / Other comments _____
_____
_____

Accuracy Assessment Form Instructions

-Italicized items can often be recorded digitally, using the GPS.

1. Enter unique number for waypoint representing center of plot.
2. Enter park code.
3. Enter Date (can enter in all sheets at end of day).
4. Enter Observer making final decision on determining dominant association for plot.
5. Enter other observer(s) who assisted or who were available for consultation for #4.
6. Enter estimated accuracy of GPS navigation to real waypoint position (can enter on all sheets at end of day if same method was used for all waypoints; enter individually in field if a point-by-point estimate was made).
7. Enter how #6 was determined (e.g., EPE reading at waypoint, 99% precisions for recorded GPS point, etc.).
8. Enter UTM Easting (in meters to nearest meter).
9. Enter UTM Northing (in meters to nearest meter).
10. UTM Zone.
11. Datum.
12. If waypoint could not be reached, enter distance (to nearest meter) and bearing (to nearest degree) from your final recorded position to the waypoint. (Alternatively, enter distance in meters easting and in meters northing (be sure to record positive or negative meters) from waypoint.
13. Record vegetation association dominating (occupying most area of) plot (plot is circular (40 meters in radius for 0.5 hectare minimum mapping unit), with waypoint at center). If you are not sure to which association it best fits, list the most likely association here and other possible associations in 14 and 15, as applicable. Association abbreviations are listed on next page.
14. If more than one association is detected within the plot (i.e., a vegetation stand "boundary" occurs within the plot, record the second most dominant association. Alternatively, if the vegetation within the plot is homogeneous, but you are not sure to which association it best fits, list the second most likely association here. If you use this entry, explain which situation you have in #19.
15. If more than one association is detected within the plot (i.e., a vegetation stand "boundary" occurs within the plot, record the third most dominant association (if applicable). Alternatively, if the vegetation within the plot is homogeneous, but you are not sure to which association it best fits, list the third most likely association here (if applicable). If you use this entry, explain which situation you have in #19.
16. List the most abundant, frequent, and/or characteristic species (Latin names) in the tree layer (suggest 1-5 species). Mark names of species that are significantly more abundant than the others (i.e., strongly dominant) with an asterisk (*).
17. List the most abundant, frequent, and/or characteristic species (Latin names) in the shrub layer (suggest 1-5 species). Mark names of species that are significantly more abundant than the others (i.e., strongly dominant) with an asterisk (*).
18. List the most abundant, frequent, and/or characteristic species (Latin names) in the herbaceous layer (suggest 1-5 species). Mark names of species that are significantly more abundant than the others (i.e., strongly dominant) with an asterisk (*).
19. Use this space to make comments on #14 or 15 or on other items that are confusing or require more detailed explanation (continue on back of form, if necessary).

APPENDIX C: Dichotomous Key to FOLS Plant Associations

Key to Natural and Semi-Natural Plant Communities at Fort Larned National Historic Site.

1a. Plant community dominated by trees..**2**
1b. Plant community dominated by herbaceous vegetation. If woody plants are present, they are scattered individuals and do not create a canopy...**3**

2a. Woodland or forest dominated by tall old trees of a single species. Leaves bright green and largely triangular, bark furrowed (Cottonwood, *Populus deltoides*). Understory composed largely of woody vines. Located surrounding the dry former oxbow at FOLS.................
Eastern Cottonwood - Black Willow Forest CEGL002018

2b. Woodland or forest of trees of mixed species, mixed heights, and mixed ages. Understory includes small shrubs, woody vines, grasses, and annual and biennial herbs. Located along the Pawnee River at FOLS...
Green Ash - Elm - Hackberry Forest CEGL002014

3a. Vegetation in mud, muck, or standing water ....
Hydrologically Disturbed Seasonal Polygonum Vegetation

3b. Upland plant communities. **4**

4a. Prairie dog holes nearby, land not previously plowed for agriculture. Located at the Santa Fe Ruts Remote Unit...**5**

4b. Prairie dog holes not conspicuous on the landscape, land previously plowed for agriculture. Located at the main unit of Fort Larned National Historic Site **6**

5a. Vegetation primarily perennial grasses over 0.5 m tall. ....
Big Bluestem-Yellow Indiangrass Western Great Plains Herbaceous Vegetation (Native Tallgrass Prairie) CEGL001464

5b. Vegetation less than 0.5 m, primarily annual grasses and annual forbs, prairie dog holes abundant...
Prairie Dog Dominated Vegetation V.D.2.N

   Subtypes
   • Vegetation dominated by multiple species of forbs...............**PD.W Prairie Dog Weeds**
   • Vegetation dominated by a fine-leaved grass (blades 3 mm or less wide) growing in tufts, with three sharp awns when in fruit......................................**PD.A Prairie Dog Aristida**
   • Vegetation dominated by bright green, coarse grass (blades usually 5-10 mm wide) with flowers in compact spikes.......................................**PD.S Prairie Dog Setaria**

6a. Dominated by perennial grasses, at least 80% of the area covered in grass........**7**

6b. Dominated by forb vegetation and annual grass vegetation ....
Old Field Weedy Herbaceous Vegetation

Subtypes:
- Vegetation a mix of weedy species..**W1.F Fine Mosaic**
- Vegetation dominated by a single species, many branched and sharp, forming dense, shrub-like stands, up to 2 m tall at maturity. Leaves simple. Inflorescences inconspicuous...**W1.K Kochia**
- Vegetation dominated by a single species, with lacy dissected leaves and white flowers arranged in umbels. New growth often a mat of basal leaves among dried hollow stalks of dead individuals. Plants grow to 2 m tall at maturity and thrive in seasonally wet areas ....**W1.C Conium**

7a. Grass fine textured and maintained by mowing to heights less than 15 cm, a landscaped rather than a native community..
Buffalo Grass Lawn

7b. Grass 30cm and taller...**8**

8a. Nearly monotypic stands of *Bromus inermis*, a bright green grass 20-50 cm tall, green early and late in season ....
Smooth Brome *Bromus inermis* Semi-Natural Herbaceous Alliance

8b. At least 10 percent of plot covered by grasses taller than 50 cm (some reaching 2 m at flowering), often a mix of species, including the bright green brome mentioned in 8a, but not limited to it..
Planted Semi-Natural Grasses in Big Bluestem Alliance

APPENDIX D: Vegetation Association Descriptions for FOLS

NatureServe. 2006. International Ecological Classification Standard: Terrestrial Ecological Classifications. NatureServe Central Databases. Arlington, VA. U.S.A. Data current as of December 2006.

U.S. NATIONAL VEGETATION CLASSIFICATION

Fort Larned National Historic Site

December 31, 2006

By
Kansas Natural Heritage Inventory
Kansas Biological Survey
2102 Constant Ave.
Lawrence, KS 66047

And
NPS - Southern Plains Network Coordinator
P.O. Box 329, 100 Ladybird Lane
Johnson City, TX 78636

This subset of the U.S. National Classification covers vegetation associations and alliances attributed to Fort Larned National Historic Site. This classification has been developed in consultation with many individuals and agencies and incorporates information from a variety of publications and other classifications. Comments and suggestions regarding the contents of this subset should be directed to Jim Drake, Regional Vegetation Ecologist, 612-331-0729, jim_drake@natureserve.org or Heidi Sosinski, Data Manager, 830-868-7128 ext. 282, heidi_sosinski@nps.gov.

VEGETATION CATEGORY DESCRIPTIONS

Populus deltoides - Salix nigra Forest

COMMON NAME   Eastern Cottonwood - Black Willow Forest
PHYSIOGNOMIC CLASS   I   Forest
PHYSIOGNOMIC SUBCLASS   I.B   Deciduous forest
PHYSIOGNOMIC GROUP   I.B.2   Cold-deciduous forest
PHYSIOGNOMIC SUBGROUP   I.B.2.N   Natural/semi-natural cold-deciduous forest
FORMATION   I.B.2.N.d   Temporarily flooded cold-deciduous forest
ALLIANCE   *Populus deltoides* Temporarily Flooded Forest Alliance

Association Identifier: CEGL002018

RANGE

Globally

> This cottonwood - black willow forest is characteristic of the fronts and banks of most major rivers and streams throughout the Central Forest Region, extending into the northern forest particularly within the Mississippi, Ohio, and Missouri River systems, extending from Ohio west to Minnesota, southward to Oklahoma, and east to Kentucky. This community once occupied vast tracts of land along river fronts and floodplain depressions. Land clearing, ditching, and draining for conversion to cropland, and logging have eliminated much of the pre-settlement stands of this natural community (NatureServe 2006).

Fort Larned National Historic Site

> Cottonwood forest occurs at Fort Larned National Historic Site only along the banks of the former oxbow lake. Historical accounts suggest that cottonwood trees were dominant along creeks and rivers in the region, and likely grew along the Pawnee River prior to settlement. Clearing of the original trees for fuel and timber and changes in the hydrology and sediment load of the river have decreased the extent of this community along the Pawnee River.

ENVIRONMENTAL DESCRIPTION

Globally

> This community is quick to colonize newly deposited substrates adjacent to rivers, lakes, streams, and in frequently flooded, low, wet depressions in floodplains. Dynamic substrate availability caused by frequent flooding encourages the establishment and maintenance of this community type (NatureServe 2006).

Fort Larned National Historic Site

> The community is found on slopes on both sides of the former oxbow.

MOST ABUNDANT SPECIES

Globally

Strata	Species
Tree	*Populus deltoides, Salix nigra*
Woody Vine	*Toxicodendron rydbergii*
Herb	*Bidens aristosa, Symphyotrichum lanceolatum*

Fort Larned National Historic Site

Strata	Species
Tree	*Populus deltoides*
Woody Vine	*Toxicodendron rydbergii*

CHARACTERISTIC SPECIES

Fort Larned National Historic Site

Strata	Species
Tree	*Populus deltoides*

VEGETATION DESCRIPTION

Globally

This community is dominated by broadleaf deciduous trees. Canopy closure is complete, or nearly so, with few shrubs and limited tree species found in the type. The tree canopy is tall (to 30 m) and dominated by *Populus deltoides* and *Salix nigra*, although *Fraxinus pennsylvanica, Acer saccharinum, Acer negundo, Platanus occidentalis*, and *Ulmus americana* are also commonly encountered. Tree diversity is limited due to the dynamics of flooding and deposition/scouring of sediments. The subcanopy is almost exclusively *Salix nigra*. The shrub layer is conspicuously absent in many parts of the range. Herbaceous growth can be thick and lush but is often patchy and sparse (NatureServe 2006).

Fort Larned National Historic Site

Cottonwood forest is dominated by a complete canopy of tall, old cottonwoods with a near complete understory of poison ivy.

COMMENTS

Hydrologic changes in the region have led to the oxbow remaining dry throughout the season. Due to these changes, no young cottonwoods have been found in the area.

MAP CODE: T1 (Tree 1)

PLOTS: BG, BH, BI

Fraxinus pennsylvanica -Ulmus spp. - *Celtis occidentalis* Forest

COMMON NAME	Green Ash - Elm - Hackberry Forest	
PHYSIOGNOMIC CLASS	I	Forest
PHYSIOGNOMIC SUBCLASS	I.B	Deciduous forest
PHYSIOGNOMIC GROUP	I.B.2	Cold-deciduous forest
PHYSIOGNOMIC SUBGROUP	I.B.2.N	Natural/semi-natural cold-deciduous forest
FORMATION	I.B.2.N.d	Temporarily flooded cold-deciduous forest
ALLIANCE		*Fraxinus pennsylvanica - Ulmus Americana - Celtis* (*occidentalis, laevigata*) Temporarily Flooded Forest Alliance

Association Identifier: CEGL002014

RANGE

Globally

This community is found in the central United States along upper floodplain terraces of rivers and streams and in upland ravine bottoms, ranging from Ohio and Ontario west to Iowa, south to Kansas, and east to Indiana (NatureServe 2006).

Fort Larned National Historic Site

Green Ash - Elm Species Forest occurs at Fort Larned National Historic Site along the Pawnee River. It occurs on banks and terraces on both sides of the river.

ENVIRONMENTAL DESCRIPTION

Globally

Stands occur along upper floodplain terraces of rivers and streams and in upland ravine bottoms. Soils are moderately well-drained to poorly drained.

Fort Larned National Historic Site

This community occurs in soils that are primarily silts, on both steep slopes and level terraces.

MOST ABUNDANT SPECIES

Fort Larned National Historic Site

Strata	Species
Tree	*Morus alba, Acer negundo, Fraxinus pennsylvanica, Ulmus americana, Populus deltoides, Prunus americana, Salix nigra*
Herbaceous	*Conium maculatum, Phytolacca americana, Alliaria petiolata, Elymus virginicus*

CHARACTERISTIC SPECIES

Fort Larned National Historic Site

Strata	**Species**
Tree	*Morus alba, Fraxinus pennsylvanica, Acer negundo, Ulmus* spp.

VEGETATION DESCRIPTION

Globally

The vegetation has an open to closed tree canopy that is dominated by *Fraxinus pennsylvanica, Celtis occidentalis*, and *Ulmus americana*. Other tree species that may be present include *Juglans nigra, Tilia americana, Acer saccharinum, and Populus deltoides. Ulmus rubra* can be part of the subcanopy. The shrub layer in the western part of the range includes *Cornus drummondii, Ribes missouriense, Symphoricarpos occidentalis*, and *Zanthoxylum americanum*, as well as woody vines, such as *Parthenocissus vitacea, Smilax tamnoides (= Smilax hispida), Toxicodendron radicans*, and *Vitis riparia* (NatureServe 2006).

Fort Larned National Historic Site

The dominants of this community are highly variable. *Morus alba, Acer negundo, Fraxinus pennsylvanica, Populus deltoides, Ulmus rubra,* and *Ulmus americana* all dominate some plots. Small thickets of *Prunus americana* occur on slopes toward the top of the bank while *Salix nigra* occurs close to the water. The understory layer includes many weedy and invasive species including *Alliaria petiolata, Elymus virginicus, Conium maculatum,* and *Phytolacca americana*. Woody vines include *Vitis riparia* and *Toxicodendron rydbergii*.

Regional floristics suggest that this riparian forest would have been dominated by *Populus deltoides* prior to settlement. No young cottonwood trees were found during the course of the study.

MAP CODE: T2 (Tree 2)

PLOTS: BE, BF, BJ, BK, BL, BM, BV, DA

Andropogon gerardii - Sorghastrum nutans Western Great Plains Herbaceous Vegetation

COMMON NAME   Big Bluestem - Yellow Indiangrass Western Great Plains Herbaceous Vegetation

PHYSIOGNOMIC CLASS	V	Herbaceous vegetation
PHYSIOGNOMIC SUBCLASS	V.A	Perennial graminoid vegetation
PHYSIOGNOMIC GROUP	V.A.5	Temperate or subpolar grassland
PHYSIOGNOMIC SUBGROUP	V.A.5.N	Natural/semi-natural temperate or subpolar grassland
FORMATION	V.A.5.N.a	Tall sod temperate grassland
ALLIANCE	*Andropogon gerardii (Sorghastrum nutans)* Herbaceous Alliance	

Association Identifier: CEGL001464

RANGE

Globally

> This big bluestem prairie is a tallgrass, wet meadow found in the west-central Great Plains of the United States, especially the foothills of Colorado, and extending east to western Kansas and Oklahoma.

Fort Larned National Historic Site

> Remnant patches of big bluestem prairie occur along the western fence line of the remote Santa Fe Trail Ruts Site.

ENVIRONMENTAL DESCRIPTION

Globally

> Stands occur in valley bottoms and terraces along larger streams and rivers. Soils are deep, somewhat poorly drained loam to sandy loams found in alluvium. Stands require subirrigated soils to persist. It occurs along floodplains of perennial rivers on the plains or, less frequently, on cobbly loam soils along the Colorado foothills. This mesic prairie association is able to survive along the foothills because the cobbly soils are able to retain adequate moisture.

Fort Larned National Historic Site

> Patches of tall grasses occur in some of the wetter areas of the Santa Fe Trail Ruts site on silty soils.

MOST ABUNDANT SPECIES

Globally

Strata	Species
Herbaceous	*Andropogon gerardii, Sorghastrum nutans, Panicum virgatum, Agropyron smithii, Sporobolus cryptandrus*
Herbaceous	

Fort Larned National Historic Site

Strata	Species
Herbaceous	*Andropogon gerardii, Sporobolus asper, Bouteloua gracilis, Schizachyrium scoparium*

CHARACTERISTIC SPECIES

Globally

Strata	Species
Herbaceous	*Andropogon gerardii, Sorghastrum nutans, Panicum virgatum, Agropyron smithii, Desmanthus illinoensis, Glycyrrhiza lepidota*

Fort Larned National Historic Site

Strata	Species
Herbaceous	*Andropogon gerardii, Sporobolus asper, Bouteloua gracilis, Schizachyrium scoparium, Sorghastrum nutans*

VEGETATION DESCRIPTION

Globally

The vegetation is dominated by tall grasses, particularly *Andropogon gerardii* and *Sorghastrum nutans*. Other grasses include *Panicum virgatum, Pascopyrum smithii* and *Sporobolus cryptandrus*. Forbs may include *Desmanthus illinoensis* and *Glycyrrhiza lepidota* (Lauver et al. 1999, NatureServe 2006).

Fort Larned National Historic Site

At the Santa Fe Trail Ruts Site, native tall grasses occur in discrete patches, each dominated by a different tall grass (*Andropogon gerardii, Schizachyrium scoparium*, and *Sorghastrum nutans*). This is believed to be a result of the grazing history of the site. Prior to grazing by cattle the tall grasses would have been more abundant and would probably have occurred in a mosaic pattern. Intensive past grazing pressure may have reduced the tall grasses to a few scattered clumps. Current monotypic grass stands are the result of clonal growth of the few remnant clumps.

MAP CODE: NG1 (Native Grass 1)

PLOTS: AL, AM and AN

Prairie Dog Town Grassland Complex

COMMON NAME	Prairie Dog Town Grassland Complex	
FORMATION CLASS	V	Herbaceous vegetation
FORMATION SUBCLASS	V.D	Annual graminoid or forb vegetation
FORMATION GROUP	V.D.2	Temperate or subpolar annual grass or forb vegetation
FORMATION SUBGROUP	V.A.2.N	Natural/semi-natural temperate or subpolar annual grasslands or forb vegetation

RANGE

Globally

This association has been derived based on data from the Black Hills. Rangewide data has not yet been compiled.

Fort Larned National Historic Site

Prairie dog town grassland complex is found only at the remote Santa Fe Trail Ruts Site of Fort Larned National Historic Site.

ENVIRONMENTAL DESCRIPTION

Globally

This association has been derived based on data from the Black Hills. Rangewide data has not yet been compiled.

Fort Larned National Historic Site

Prairie dog town grassland complex is found on level to moderately sloping sites of all aspects on highly disturbed soil.

MOST ABUNDANT SPECIES

Globally

Strata	Species
Information not available	

Fort Larned National Historic Site

Strata	Species
Herbaceous	*Aristida oligantha, Conyza ramosissima, Kochia scoparia, Seteria pumila, Oxalis dillenii, Cirsium ochrocentrum*

CHARACTERISTIC SPECIES

Globally

Strata	Species
Information not available	

Fort Larned National Historic Site

Strata	Species
Herbaceous	*Aristida oligantha, Conyza ramosissima, Mollugo verticillata, Asclepias verticillata*

VEGETATION DESCRIPTION

Fort Larned National Historic Site

The prairie dog town is noteworthy for its short (< 20 cm) vegetation, limited diversity, and regular prairie dog holes. Prairie dogs keep sight lines open by clipping all plants, with the exception of *Cirsium ochrocentrum*. Many of the plants are annual, growing in nearly monotypic patches. In 2005, the north end of the Santa Fe Ruts Site was dominated by *Setaria pumila*, the center by *Aristida oligantha*, and the east side by a combination of *Conyza ramosissima, Kochia scoparia, Oxalis dillenii and Convolvulus arvense*.

MAP CODE: PD (Prairie Dog)

MAP UNITS
PD.A = *Aristida* dominated
PD.S = *Setaria* dominated
PD.W = Mixed Weeds

PLOTS:
PD.A = AP, AQ, BA
PD.S =   BB, BC, BD
PD.W = AO, AR, AS, AT

Planted Semi - Natural Restored Grassland Prairie

PHYSIOGNOMIC CLASS	V	Herbaceous vegetation
PHYSIOGNOMIC SUBCLASS	V.A	Perennial graminoid vegetation
PHYSIOGNOMIC GROUP	V.A.5	Temperate or subpolar grassland
PHYSIOGNOMIC SUBGROUP	V.A.5.N	Natural/semi-natural temperate or subpolar grassland
FORMATION	V.A.5.N.a	Tall sod temperate grassland
ALLIANCE	*Andropogon gerardii (Sorghastrum nutans)* Herbaceous Alliance	

Alliance Identifier: A.1192

RANGE

Globally

> This community has been defined for Fort Larned National Historic Site. At Fort Larned National Historic Site, managers are attempting to restore vegetation to the Big Bluestem (Yellow Indiangrass) Alliance through planting native grasses and forbs in formerly plowed fields. Natural vegetation of this alliance is most common in tallgrass prairies of the Great Plains. Stands of Big Bluestem (Yellow Indiangrass) Herbaceous Alliance occur from Texas and Arkansas north into Montana, and east into Michigan, Ohio, Virginia, and Tennessee. In Canada it is found in southern Saskatchewan, southern Manitoba, and southern and northwestern Ontario.

Fort Larned National Historic Site

> Planted Semi-Natural Grasslands are found in the main Fort Unit both north and south of the Pawnee River.

ENVIRONMENTAL DESCRIPTION

Fort Larned National Historic Site

> The fields that have been re-planted with native grasses were once plowed and leveled for agriculture, so they are flat with loamy soils.

MOST ABUNDANT SPECIES

Fort Larned National Historic Site

Panicum virgatum Subtype

Strata	Species
Herbaceous	*Panicum virgatum*

Sorghastrum nutans, Bouteloua curtipendula, Andropogon gerardii Subtype

Strata	Species
Herbaceous	*Bromus inermis, Sorghastrum nutans, Bouteloua curtipendula, Andropogon gerardii*

Leptochloa dubia Subtype

Strata	Species
Herbaceous	*Leptochloa dubia, Seteria viridis, Gaillardia pulchella, Bouteloua curtipendula, Chloris virgata*

CHARACTERISTIC SPECIES

Fort Larned National Historic Site

Panicum virgatum Subtype

Strata	Species
Herbaceous	*Panicum virgatum*

Sorghastrum nutans, Bouteloua curtipendula, Andropogon gerardii Subtype

Strata	Species
Herbaceous	*Sorghastrum nutans, Bouteloua curtipendula, Andropogon gerardii*

Leptochloa dubia Subtype

Strata	Species
Herbaceous	*Leptochloa dubia*

VEGETATION DESCRIPTION

Fort Larned National Historic Site

The dominant vegetation of the re-planted grasslands changes with time since planting, extent of measures to control smooth brome, and expression of the original seed mix. While the long-term goal of restoration is a fine mosaic of mixed native grass species, most fields are currently dominated by a small number of grass species.

Old stands of *Panicum virgatum* have grown into near monotypic stands of switch grass to 1.5 m tall. The *Sorghastrum nutans, Bouteloua curtipendula, Andropogon gerardii* Subtype can be predominately smooth brome (0.5 m tall), or can have mixtures of native tall grasses to 2 m in height. In 2005, one restored field was inadvertently seeded with green sprangletop (*Leptochloa dubia*) which was the dominant grass at the time of the field survey. Fort Larned administrators hope that the winters, which are longer and colder in Kansas than in the grass's native Texas, will check the growth of this grass, and that the co-planted bluestem grasses will begin to dominate. However, at the time of writing, the prevalence of *Leptochloa* made this subtype distinct from the other re-planted grasslands.

Many of the restored grassland fields contain wildflower species native to the Great Plains but not otherwise found at Fort Larned National Historic Site including *Salvia azurea, Gaillardia pulchella, Ratibida columnifera* and *Helianthus maximiliani.*

MAP CODE: PG1

MAP UNITS
PG1.L = *Leptochloa dubia* Subtype
PG1.M = *Sorghastrum, Bouteloua, Andropogon* Subtype
PG1.P = *Panicum virgatum* Subtype

PLOTS:
PG1.L = DO, DP, DQ
PG1.M   = AC, AD, AE, AF, BN, BO, BP, DH, DJ, DK
PG1.P = BW, DF

Old Field Weedy Herbaceous Vegetation

FORMATION CLASS	V	Herbaceous vegetation
FORMATION SUBCLASS	V.D	Annual graminoid or forb vegetation
FORMATION GROUP	V.D.2	Temperate or subpolar annual grass or forb vegetation
FORMATION SUBGROUP	V.A.2.N	Natural/semi-natural temperate or subpolar annual grasslands or forb vegetation

Vegetation Type First Described for Fort Larned National Historic Site

RANGE

Globally

> This type has been defined for Fort Larned National Historic Site, but is presumed to be a widespread community of disturbed habitats. It would include the *Kochia scoparia/Bromus* spp. Early Seral Community as defined for Scotts Bluff National Monument.

Fort Larned National Historic Site

> This community occurs in anthropogenically disturbed areas of the main unit of Fort Larned National Historic Site, including the historic dump site, the oxbow island, and the low-lying areas along the Pawnee River floodplain.

> Three subtypes have been identified:
> > *Conium maculatum* Subtype (Poison Hemlock Subtype)
> > *Kochia scoparia* Subtype (Mexican Firebush Subtype)
> > Fine Mosaic Subtype

ENVIRONMENTAL DESCRIPTION

Fort Larned National Historic Site

> Old Field Weedy Vegetation occurs on flat to moderate slopes of all aspects on soils that are primarily silty loams.

> *Conium maculatum* Subtype is confined primarily to low-lying areas and can be found in temporarily flooded areas.

> *Kochia scoparia* Subtype and Fine Mosaic Subtype occur throughout.

MOST ABUNDANT SPECIES

Fort Larned National Historic Site
    Conium maculatum Subtype

Strata	**Species**
Herbaceous	*Conium maculatum*

    Kochia scoparia Subtype

Strata	**Species**
Herbaceous	*Kochia scoparia, Bromus japonicus*

    Fine Mosaic Subtype

Strata	**Species**
Herbaceous	*Bromus japonicus, Rumex altissimus, Ambrosia psilostachya, Bromus inermis, Kochia scoparia, Bromus tectorum, Andropogon gerardii, Agropyron smithii*

CHARACTERISTIC SPECIES

Fort Larned National Historic Site
    Conium maculatum Subtype

Strata	**Species**
Herbaceous	*Conium maculatum*

    Kochia scoparia Subtype

Strata	**Species**
Herbaceous	*Kochia scoparia, Bromus japonicus*

    Fine Mosaic Subtype

Strata	**Species**
Herbaceous	*Bromus japonicus, Ambrosia psilostachya, Bromus tectorum*

VEGETATION DESCRIPTION

Fort Larned National Historic Site
    Old Field Weedy Herbaceous vegetation is highly variable. Generally dominated by mid-height introduced grasses (0.5 m) and tall annual forbs (to 2 m), local patches may contain small early successional trees (such as *Gleditsia triacanthos*) and native grasses (including *Andropogon gerardii, Agropyron smithii*, and *Sporobolus asper*). Old Field Weedy Vegetation plots have in common a high percentage of annual species cover (> 30%) and a high percentage of forb cover relative to surrounding fields of smooth brome and restored grassland.

Within this community, monotypic stands of *Kochia scoparia* and *Conium maculatum* exist. Where these stands are large enough to map, they have been mapped as distinct subtypes. However, as both *Kochia* and *Conium* are annual early seral species, locations of these subtypes are not expected to remain constant.

MAP CODE: W1 (Weeds 1)

MAP UNITS
W1.C = *Conium* Subtype
W1.F =   Fine Mosaic Subtype
W1.K = *Kochia* Subtype

PLOTS:
W1.C: BX
W1.F: AU, BQ, BR, BS, BT, BU, BY, DE
W1.K: AA, AV, BZ

Bromus inermis Semi-Natural Herbaceous Alliance

COMMON NAME   Smooth Brome Semi-Natural Vegetation
PHYSIOGNOMIC CLASS   V   Herbaceous vegetation
PHYSIOGNOMIC SUBCLASS   V.A   Perennial graminoid vegetation
PHYSIOGNOMIC GROUP   V.A.5   Temperate or subpolar grassland
PHYSIOGNOMIC SUBGROUP   V.A.5.N   Natural/semi-natural temperate or subpolar grassland
FORMATION   V.A.5.N.d   Medium-tall bunch temperate or subpolar grassland
ALLIANCE   *Bromus inermis* Semi-Natural Herbaceous Alliance

Alliance Identifier: A.3561

RANGE

Globally

> This introduced-species grassland alliance occurs throughout the Northern Great Plains in a variety of human-disturbed habitats.

Fort Larned National Historic Site

> At Fort Larned National Historic Site, Smooth Brome Vegetation dominates the areas of the main unit formerly used for agriculture. The introduced grass species is also present in many re-planted and restored fields on Fort Larned National Historic Site, but where possible these areas were classified according to the native grasses that had been re-planted.

ENVIRONMENTAL DESCRIPTION

Globally

> This introduced-species grassland alliance occurs widely throughout the Northern Great Plains of the United States, and perhaps more widely in the Midwest and Canada. It likely occurs throughout much of the Rocky Mountains and Intermountain West. In semi-arid environments, it is restricted to relatively mesic conditions such as in riparian areas or forest openings at montane elevations. Stands can occur in a wide variety of human-disturbed habitats, including highway rights-of-way, jeep trails, etc. *Bromus inermis* is also widely planted for cover, pasture, and hay, and has escaped into a variety of habitats (NatureServe 2006).

Fort Larned National Historic Site

> Smooth Brome Vegetation grows on fields previously leveled and plowed for agriculture. The slope is flat and the soils are loamy, at least near the surface.

MOST ABUNDANT SPECIES

Globally

Strata	Species
Herbaceous	*Bromus inermis, Agropyron smithii, Stipa comata*

Fort Larned National Historic Site

Strata	Species
Herbaceous	*Bromus inermis, Convolvulus arvense, Kochia scoparia, Setaria pumila*

CHARACTERISTIC SPECIES

Globally

Strata	Species
Herbaceous	*Bromus inermis, Agropyron smithii, Stipa comata*

Fort Larned National Historic Site

Strata	Species
Herbaceous	*Bromus inermis, Convolvulus arvense, Kochia scoparia, Setaria pumila*

VEGETATION DESCRIPTION

Globally

This alliance is characterized by a moderately dense to dense layer of medium-tall (0.5-1 m) perennial graminoids. The dominant grass is *Bromus inermis*, a naturalized species from Eurasia. Other weedy species may occur as well, but native species are generally less than 10% cover. Native species may include mixed-grass prairie grasses, such as *Agropyron smithii* and *Hesperostipa comata (= Stipa comata)*, as well as others. Where native species are conspicuous enough to identify the native plant association that could occupy the site, the stand has been typed as such (NatureServe 2006).

Fort Larned National Historic Site

Smooth brome, an introduced cool-season grass from Eurasia, grows 0.3 to 1 m tall, and entirely covers more than 90% of the plots. Other weeds found in association with smooth brome include *Convolvulus arvense, Kochia scoparia* and *Setaria pumila*. Native grasses cover less than 10% of the plots, but can include *Bouteloua curtipendula, Sorghastrum nutans* and *Andropogon gerardii*.

MAP CODE: PG2 (Planted Grass 2)

PLOTS: AB, AG, AH, AI, AW, DG, DL, DM, DN

Hydrologically Disturbed Seasonal *Polygonum* Vegetation

COMMON NAME   Smartweed species Seasonally Flooded Herbaceous Alliance

PHYSIOGNOMIC CLASS	V	Herbaceous vegetation
PHYSIOGNOMIC SUBCLASS	V.B	Perennial forb vegetation
PHYSIOGNOMIC GROUP	V.B.2	Temperate or subpolar perennial forb vegetation
PHYSIOGNOMIC SUBGROUP	V.B.2.N	Natural/semi-natural temperate or subpolar perennial forb vegetation
FORMATION	V.B.2.N.h	Seasonally flooded temperate perennialforb vegetation

ALLIANCE   *Polygonum* spp. (section Persicaria) Seasonally Flooded Herbaceous Alliance

Alliance Identifier: A. 1881

Vegetation Type First Described for Fort Larned National Historic Site

RANGE

Globally

> While the Smartweed species Seasonally Flooded Herbaceous Alliance is widespread, it has not been described for the natural areas of Kansas. This type is currently defined only at Fort Larned National Historic Site, where the hydrology has been substantially altered by human agriculture and road building.

Fort Larned National Historic Site

> Hydrologically Disturbed Seasonal Polygonum Vegetation occurs in and along the Pawnee River bottom in the main unit of Fort Larned National Historic Site and where a small drainage has been impounded by the roadbed on the west side of the remote Santa Fe Trail Ruts Site.

ENVIRONMENTAL DESCRIPTION

Globally

> In the southeastern United States, this alliance occurs in a wide variety of human- and beaver-created wetlands (wet depressions, lakes, and ponds), including a band ringing the shores of ponds in the East Gulf Coastal Plain and in ditches and sloughs in the Mississippi River Alluvial Plain. In the western United States, Great Plains, and one province in Canada, it occurs over a wide elevational range from near sea level to over 2700 m. Stands are found in permanently flooded depressions such as margins of lake shores and oxbow lakes in river floodplains. It occurs in shallow water along the edges of ponds and lakes in the western United States. Stands are found in oxbow lakes and backwater areas of the Columbia River floodplain, in glacial ponds, or prairie potholes, in northern Montana, and in shallow lakes in the mountains of Colorado. Stands are located in standing water that is permanent or present at least during the growing season. These ponds have low concentrations of ions and salts and bottoms composed of finer

sediments, organic muck, clay, or silt. The elevation of the vegetation in the alliance varies depending on geographical location. Stands on the Columbia River are located just above sea level, in Montana between 640-1080 m, and in Colorado from 2050-2700 m. *Typha latifolia* and *Schoenoplectus acutus* may grow adjacent to the vegetation in this alliance in deeper water, and *Carex aquatilis* grows in shallower water along the shore. (NatureServe 2006)

Fort Larned National Historic Site
> Damming of the Pawnee River upstream and downstream from FOLS has led to silt accumulation and seasonal standing water in the river bed. Water depth can vary from 0 to 1 m. Depending on the water depth and clarity, smartweed vegetation can be found seasonally in all but the deepest channel of the river bed. Soils are silty and mucky.
>
> At the Santa Fe Trail Ruts Site, a small drainage blocked by the roadbed leads to seasonally wet conditions.

MOST ABUNDANT SPECIES

Fort Larned National Historic Site

Strata	Species
Herbaceous	*Polygonum lapathifolium, Polygonum bicorne, Conium maculatum, Rumex altissimus*

CHARACTERISTIC SPECIES

Fort Larned National Historic Site

Strata	Species
Herbaceous	*Polygonum lapathifolium, Polygonum bicorne, Rumex altissimus*

VEGETATION DESCRIPTION

Fort Larned National Historic Site
> In the Pawnee River, the vegetation grows 1 to 2 m tall and only covers 60 to 80 percent of the surface. In areas of deeper water, only *Polygonum* species grow, while areas closer to the shore also support *Conium maculatum*, *Rumex crispus*, and *Conyza canadensis*.
>
> In the *Polygonum* community at the Santa Fe Trail Ruts Site, there is little bare ground or standing water. Other than a few annual sunflowers (*Helianthus annuus*) along the fence, the vegetation is less than 1 m. tall.

MAP CODE: W2 (Weeds 2)

PLOTS: AJ, AK, DB, DC, DD

Buffalo Grass Lawn
Buchloe dactyloides Planted/Cultivated Herbaceous Vegetation

COMMON NAME   Buffalo Grass Planted/Cultivated Herbaceous Vegetation
PHYSIOGNOMIC CLASS   V   Herbaceous vegetation
PHYSIOGNOMIC SUBCLASS   V.A   Perennial graminoid vegetation
PHYSIOGNOMIC GROUP   V.A.5   Temperate or subpolar grassland
FORMATION   V.A.5.C.b   Landscaped urban/suburban/rural
                                                   temperate or subpolar grassland.

RANGE

Globally
> Comprised of a species native to the Western Great Plains, Buffalo Grass lawns have been planted across the Great Plains.

Fort Larned National Historic Site
> Buffalo Grass Lawn surrounds the historic fort itself and has been planted in the picnic and parking areas.

ENVIRONMENTAL DESCRIPTION

Fort Larned National Historic Site
> This community occurs on level ground over compacted soils. It is maintained by regular mowing.

MOST ABUNDANT SPECIES

Fort Larned National Historic Site

Strata	Species
Herbaceous	*Buchloe dactyloides, Digitaria sanguinalis, Taraxacum officinale*

CHARACTERISTIC SPECIES

Fort Larned National Historic Site

Strata	Species
Herbaceous	*Buchloe dactyloides, Digitaria sanguinalis*

VEGETATION DESCRIPTION

Fort Larned National Historic Site
> Regular mowing to a low height (< 10 cm) keeps the buffalo grass dominant in the lawn surrounding the fort, adjacent to the parking lot, and in the picnic ground. The patches immediately south of the fort contain a greater mix of grasses, but Fort Larned National Historic Site's administration hopes to encourage buffalo grass through regular short mowing.

MAP CODE: G2   PLOTS: CA

REFERENCES

Association, G. P. F. 1986. <u>Flora of the Great Plains</u>. Lawrence, Kansas, University Press of Kansas.

Daubenmire, R. 1959. A Canopy-Coverage Method of Vegetational Analysis. Northwest Science 33(1): 42-65.

Grossman D.H., D. Faber-Langendoen, A.S. Weakley, M. Anderson, P. Bourgeron, R. Crawford, K. Goodin, S. Landaal, K. Metzler, K.D. Patterson, M. Pyne, M. Reid, and L. Sneddon. 1998. International classification of ecological communities: terrestrial vegetation of the United States. Volume I, The National Vegetation Classification System: development, status, and applications. The Nature Conservancy: Arlington, VA.

Grossman, D.H., K.L. Goodin, X. Li, D. Faber-Langendoen, M. Anderson, and R. Vaughan, Establishing standards for field methods and mapping procedures. 1994. Prepared for the USGS-NPS Vegetation Mapping Program by The Nature Conservancy, Arlington VA, and Environmental Science Research Institute, Redlands, CA.

Lauver, C.L., K. Kindscher, D. Faber-Langendoen, and R. Schneider. 1999. A classification of the natural vegetation of Kansas. The Southwestern Naturalist 44:421-443.

NatureServe. 2006. NatureServe Explorer: An online encyclopedia of life [web application]. Version 4.7. NatureServe, Arlington, Virginia. Available http://www.natureserve.org/explorer. (Accessed: May 24, 2006).

APPENDIX E: FOLS Species List

This is not a complete list for FOLS. This list only contains the species recorded for the 2005 sample plots and the 2006 accuracy assessment points. Genus-only records indicate an unknown species.

Family	Scientific Name	Common Name
Aceraceae	*Acer negundo*	boxelder
Amaranthaceae	*Amaranthus palmeri*	carelessweed
Anacardiaceae	*Toxicodendron radicans*	eastern poison ivy
	Toxicodendron rydbergii	western poison ivy
Apiaceae	*Conium maculatum*	poison hemlock
Apocynaceae	*Apocynum cannabinum*	Indianhemp
Asclepiadaceae	*Asclepias pumila*	plains milkweed
	Asclepias stenophylla	slimleaf milkweed
	Asclepias syriaca	common milkweed
	Asclepias verticillata	whorled milkweed
	Cynanchum laeve	honeyvine
Asteraceae	*Ambrosia grayi*	woollyleaf burr ragweed
	Ambrosia psilostachya	western ragweed
	Ambrosia trifida	great ragweed
	Aster falcatus	
	Brickellia eupatorioides var. eupatorioides	false boneset
	Cirsium arvense	Canada thistle
	Cirsium ochrocentrum	yellowspine thistle
	Cirsium undulatum	wavyleaf thistle
	Cirsium vulgare	bull thistle
	Conyza canadensis	Canadian horseweed
	Conyza ramosissima	dwarf horseweed
	Coreopsis tinctoria	golden tickseed
	Gaillardia pulchella	firewheel
	Helianthus annuus	common sunflower
	Helianthus maximiliani	Maximilian sunflower
	Lactuca serriola	prickly lettuce
	Liatris punctata	dotted blazing star
	Ratibida columnifera	upright prairie coneflower
	Ratibida tagetes	green prairie coneflower
	Simsia calva	awnless bushsunflower
	Solidago gigantea	giant goldenrod
	Solidago mollis	velvety goldenrod
	Solidago nemoralis	gray goldenrod
	Taraxacum officinale	common dandelion
	Tragopogon dubius	yellow salsify
	Vernonia baldwinii	Baldwin's ironweed
	Xanthium strumarium var. strumarium	rough cockleburr
Brassicaceae	*Alliaria petiolata*	garlic mustard
Cannabaceae	*Cannabis sativa ssp. indica*	marijuana

Caprifoliaceae	*Symphoricarpos orbiculatus*	coralberry
Chenopodiaceae	*Chenopodium album*	lambsquarters
	Chenopodium berlandieri	pitseed goosefoot
	Chenopodium simplex	mapleleaf goosefoot
	Kochia scoparia	Mexican-fireweed
	Salsola kali	Russian thistle
Convolvulaceae	*Convolvulus arvensis*	field bindweed
Cucurbitaceae	*Cucurbita foetidissima*	Missouri gourd
Cupressaceae	*Juniperus virginiana*	eastern redcedar
Cyperaceae	*Cyperus lupulinus*	Great Plains flatsedge
Euphorbiaceae	*Chamaesyce maculata*	
	Euphorbia dentata	
	Euphorbia maculata	
	Euphorbia marginata	snow on the mountain
	Euphorbia prostrata	
Fabaceae	*Amorpha canescens*	leadplant
	Amorpha fruticosa	desert false indigo
	Astragalus mollissimus	woolly locoweed
	Cassia chamaecrista	
	Dalea purpurea	violet prairie clover
	Desmanthus illinoensis	prairie bundleflower
	Gleditsia triacanthos	honeylocust
	Glycyrrhiza lepidota	American licorice
	Melilotus officinalis	yellow sweetclover
	Trifolium repens	white clover
Lamiaceae	*Nepeta cataria*	catnip
	Salvia azurea	azure blue sage
	Salvia reflexa	lanceleaf sage
	Teucrium canadense	Canada germander
	Teucrium canadense var. canadense	Canada germander
Malvaceae	*Abutilon theophrasti*	velvetleaf
	Callirhoe involucrata	purple poppymallow
	Sphaeralcea coccinea	scarlet globemallow
Menispermaceae	*Cocculus carolinus*	Carolina coralbead
Molluginaceae	*Mollugo verticillata*	green carpetweed
Moraceae	*Maclura pomifera*	osage orange
	Morus alba	white mulberry
	Morus rubra	red mulberry
Nyctaginaceae	*Mirabilis linearis*	narrowleaf four o'clock
	Mirabilis nyctaginea	heartleaf four o'clock
Oleaceae	*Fraxinus americana*	white ash
	Fraxinus pennsylvanica	green ash
	Fraxinus velutina	velvet ash
Oxalidaceae	*Oxalis dillenii*	
	Oxalis stricta	common yellow oxalis
Papaveraceae	*Argemone polyanthemos*	crested pricklypoppy
Phytolaccaceae	*Phytolacca americana*	American pokeweed
	Phytolacca americana var. americana	American pokeweed

Poaceae	*Andropogon gerardii*	big bluestem
	Aristida oligantha	prairie threeawn
	Bothriochloa bladhii	Caucasian bluestem
	Bothriochloa saccharoides	silver bluestem
	Bouteloua curtipendula	sideoats grama
	Bouteloua gracilis	blue grama
	Bromus inermis	smooth brome
	Bromus japonicus	Japanese brome
	Bromus tectorum	cheatgrass
	Buchloe dactyloides	buffalograss
	Cenchrus longispinus	mat sandbur
	Chloris verticillata	tumble windmill grass
	Chloris virgata	feather fingergrass
	Digitaria ischaemum	smooth crabgrass
	Elymus virginicus	Virginia wildrye
	Eragrostis cilianensis	stinkgrass
	Leptochloa dubia	green sprangletop
	Muhlenbergia bushii	nodding muhly
	Panicum capillare	witchgrass
	Panicum virgatum	switchgrass
	Pascopyrum smithii	western wheatgrass
	Pennisetum glaucum	pearl millet
	Poa pratensis	Kentucky bluegrass
	Schizachyrium scoparium	little bluestem
	Setaria parviflora	yellow bristlegrass
	Setaria pumila	yellow bristlegrass
	Setaria viridis	green bristlegrass
	Sorghastrum nutans	Indiangrass
	Sorghum halepense	Johnsongrass
	Sporobolus compositus var. compositus	composite dropseed
	Sporobolus coromandelianus	Madagascar dropseed
	Sporobolus cryptandrus	sand dropseed
	Tridens flavus	purpletop tridens
Polygonaceae	*Polygonum arenarium*	European knotweed
	Polygonum arenastrum	oval-leaf knotweed
	Polygonum bicorne	=*Polygonum pensylvanicum*
	Polygonum lapathifolium	curlytop knotweed
	Polygonum pensylvanicum	Pennsylvania smartweed
	Polygonum scandens	climbing false buckwheat
	Rumex altissimus	pale dock
	Rumex crispus	curly dock
Portulacaceae	*Portulaca oleracea*	little hogweed
Rosaceae	*Coleogyne ramosissima*	blackbrush
	Prunus americana	American plum
Rubiaceae	*Cephalanthus occidentalis*	common buttonbush
Salicaceae	*Populus deltoides*	eastern cottonwood
	Salix amygdaloides	peachleaf willow
	Salix nigra	black willow

Scrophulariaceae	*Verbascum thapsus*	common mullein
Solanaceae	*Physalis longifolia*	longleaf groundcherry
	Solanum rostratum	buffalobur nightshade
Ulmaceae	*Celtis laevigata*	sugarberry
	Ulmus americana	American elm
	Ulmus pumila	Siberian elm
	Ulmus rubra	slippery elm
Vitaceae	*Vitis riparia*	riverbank grape
Zygophyllaceae	*Tribulus terrestris*	puncturevine

APPENDIX F: Photo Interpretation Mapping Conventions and Visual Key

Fort Larned National Historic Site - Map Units

This section describes the map units for the Fort Larned National Historic Site Vegetation Mapping Project. Its purpose is to:

- Describe the vegetation of each map unit;
- Provide a ground photo image for each map unit;
- Describe the link between each map unit and the U.S. National Vegetation Classification;
- Provide visual examples of each map unit with aerial photographs and delineated overlays.

The map units for FOLS were based on a combination of NVC plant associations/alliances, local requests (i.e. Park Specials), the limitations of the digital imagery, and land-use / land-cover classes. The vegetation described in this section reflects the classification designed specifically for this project. Lookup tables that include the names of each code are included on the DVD. Non-vegetated map units are not described in this key.

Each map unit is described by a variety of characteristics and features. These include vegetation descriptions, a ground photograph and typical digital imagery signatures taken from the 2005 true color NAIP digital orthophoto and the 2005 color infrared KU digital orthophoto used as basemaps for this project. Many of the map unit descriptions rely heavily on the corresponding vegetation descriptions for the associations/alliances provided by NatureServe. Each map unit is typically made up of one vegetation association or alliance as listed. The sample ground photographs are from a variety of sources including ground photos of the sample plots and photos taken during signature verification trips or provided by KSHNI.

Forests and Woodlands

F-CTBW   *Populus deltoides - Salix nigra* Forest
Eastern Cottonwood - Black Willow Forest

Associations and Alliances
Populus deltoides - Salix nigra Forest

Common Species
Populus deltoides
Salix nigra
Toxicodendron rydbergii

Range and Distribution

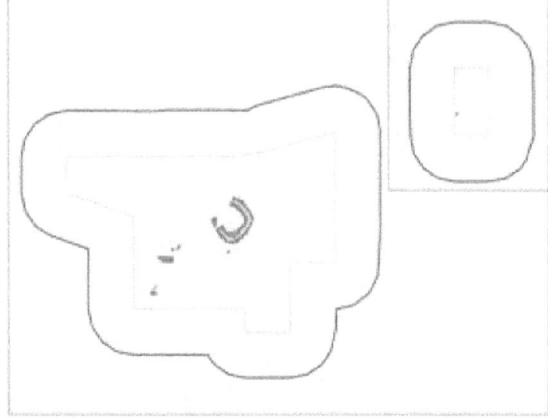

Description
Cottonwood forests occur at FOLS only along the banks of the former oxbow lake and in small patches along the Pawnee River. It is likely that this type was once more prevalent but clearing for fuel and timber changed the hydrology and sediment load decreasing the extent of this community. This type and its associated species are tied directly to the dynamics of flooding and deposition/scouring of sediments by the river. Hydrologic changes in the region have led to the oxbow remaining dry throughout the season. Due to these changes, no young cottonwoods have been found in the area. Where it was found this type was dominated by a complete canopy of broadleaf deciduous trees including tall, old cottonwoods and black willow with a near complete understory of poison ivy. Other deciduous trees common to the green ash map unit were sometimes encountered in this type. This overlap in species probably caused some confusion in the mapping. The shrub layer is conspicuously absent in some of the stands at FOLS and the herbaceous layer can be thick and lush but is often patchy and sparse. On the true color imagery this type appeared as fluffy, light green trees with larger crowns than the green ash type.

Photo Signature Examples

Representative Ground Photo

F-GASH   *Fraxinus pennsylvanica - Ulmus* spp. *- Celtis occidentalis* Forest
Green Ash - Elm - Common Hackberry Forest

Associations and Alliances
Fraxinus pennsylvanica - Ulmus spp. *- Celtis occidentalis* Forest

Common Species
Morus alba
Fraxinus pennsylvanica
Acer negundo
Ulmus spp.

Range and Distribution

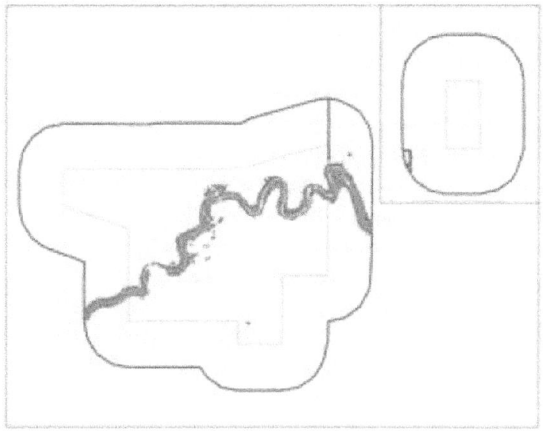

Description
This is a common forest map class found at FOLS extensively along the Pawnee River. It occurs on banks and terraces on both sides of the river. The dominants of this community are highly variable and some areas contain cottonwood trees that appeared similar on the photos. This similarity may have led to some confusion in the mapping. Small thickets of plum (*Prunus americana*) occurred on slopes toward the top of the bank while black willow (*Salix nigra*) occurred closer to the water. The understory layer included many weedy and invasive species and some woody vines. It is thought that this riparian forest may have been dominated by cottonwoods prior to settlement. No young cottonwood trees were found during the course of the study. On the imagery this type has smaller trees than do cottonwood stands having a representative dark green, textured signature.

Photo Signature Examples

Representative Ground Photo

Herbaceous Vegetation

H-BIGB	*Andropogon gerardii - Sorghastrum nutans* W. Great Plains Herbaceous Veg.
	Big Bluestem – Yellow Indiangrass W. Great Plains Herbaceous Vegetation

Associations and Alliances

Andropogon gerardii - Sorghastrum nutans
Western Great Plains Herbaceous Vegetation

Common Species

Andropogon gerardii
Sporobolus asper
Bouteloua gracilis
Schizyachrium scoparius
Sorghastrum nutans

Range and Distribution

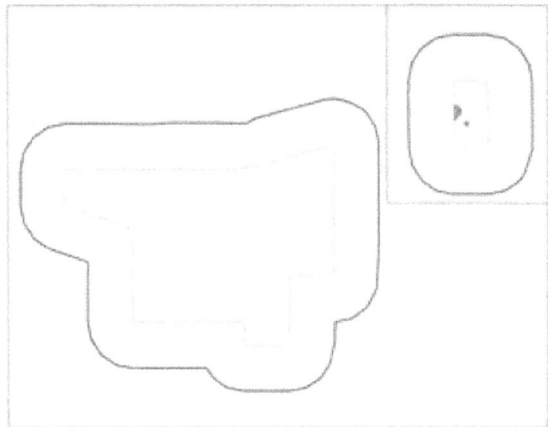

Description

This type represents the remnant patches of big bluestem prairie that occurred along the western fence line at the Santa Fe Trail Ruts Site. Although this type has some of the same species as the restored prairie type it is thought to be natural stands that have not been planted. At some point the restored prairie areas may be better classified as this type. At the rut site the small patches of this type occurred in some of the wetter areas on silty soils. On the true color imagery this type had a smooth, dark green signature.

Photo Signature Examples

Representative Ground Photo

H-BUFO *Buchloe dactyloides* **Planted/Cultivated Herbaceous Vegetation**
Buffalo Grass Herbaceous Alliance

Associations and Alliances
Buchloe dactyloides Planted/Cultivated Herbaceous Vegetation

Common Species
Buchloe dactyloides
Digitaria sanguinalis
Taraxacum officinale

Range and Distribution

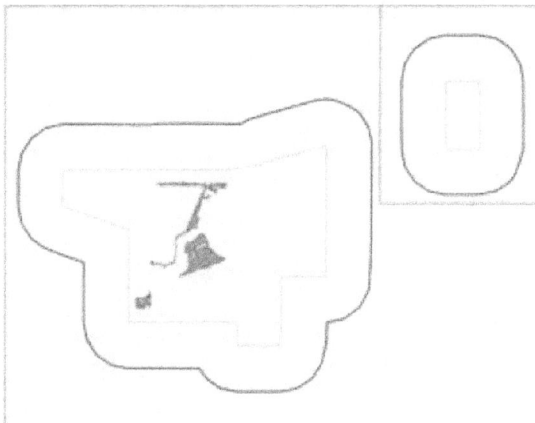

Description
This type represents the maintained lawns and pathways at FOLS. Buffalo grass lawns surround the historic fort and have been planted in the picnic and parking areas. Regular mowing to a low height (< 10 cm) keeps the buffalo grass dominant in most areas but patches immediately south of the fort contain a greater mix of grasses. On the color infrared imagery this type appeared as smooth, mottled signature. The prevalent colors were a light blue-green with red splotches that corresponded to small stands of forbs.

Photo Signature Examples

Representative Ground Photo

H-PDOG   Prairie Dog Town Grassland Complex

Associations and Alliances
Prairie Dog Town Grassland Complex

Common Species
Aristida oligantha
Conyza ramosissima
Kochia scoparia
Seteria pumila
Oxalis dillenii
Cirsium ochrocentrum
Mollugo verticillata
Asclepias verticillata

Range and Distribution

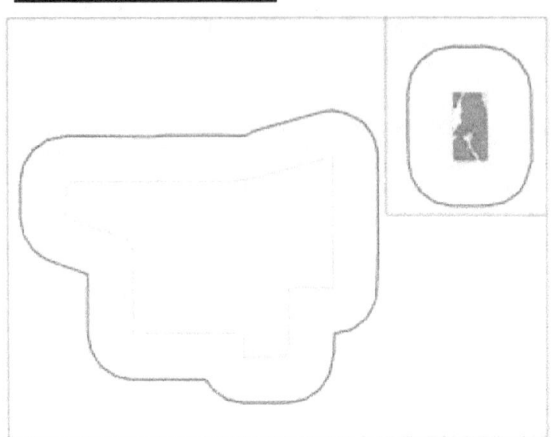

Description
This type was only found on the Santa Fe Trail Ruts Site. The prairie dog town here is noteworthy for its short (< 20 cm) vegetation, limited diversity, and regular-spaced prairie dog holes. Prairie dogs kept sight lines open by clipping all plants, with the exception of *Cirsium ochrocentrum*. Many of the plants were annual, growing in nearly monotypic patches. In 2005, the north end of the Santa Fe Ruts Site was dominated by *Setaria pumila*, the center by *Aristida oligantha*, and the east side by a combination of *Conyza ramosissima, Kochia scoparia, Oxalis dillenii* and *Convolvulus arvense*. On both sets of imagery this type contained a very characteristic signature consisting of an intricate patchwork of lines and holes. This type was mapped to the extent of the disturbance caused by the prairie dogs.

Photo Signature Examples

Representative Ground Photo

H-REPR   *Andropogon gerardii - (Sorghastrum nutans)* Herbaceous Alliance
Planted Semi - Natural Restored Grassland Prairie

Associations and Alliances
Andropogon gerardii - (Sorghastrum nutans)
Herbaceous Alliance

Common Species
Panicum virgatum
Sorghastrum nutans
Bouteloua curtipendula
Andropogon gerardii
Bromus inermis

Range and Distribution

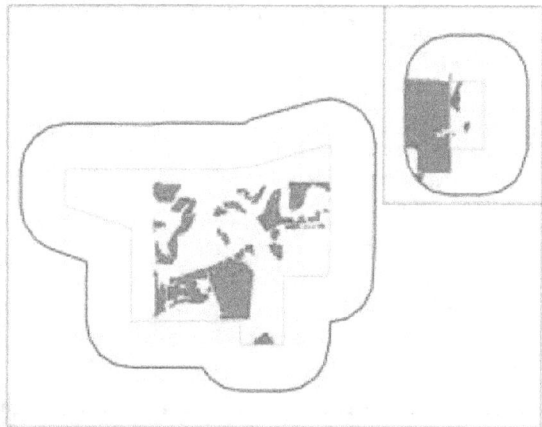

Description
This type represents the active restoration of native tall grass prairie at FOLS, where the managers are attempting to restore non-native and introduced vegetation. This is being accomplished through a regime of herbicide, planting and periodic burning in the formerly plowed fields. The dominant vegetation of this type will likely change with time depending on the extent of the control measures and the expression of the original seed mix. While the long-term goal is a fine mosaic of mixed native grass species, most fields are currently dominated by a small number of grass species. Depending on the species composition three subtypes were identified at FOLS. These included: the *Panicum virgatum*, the *Sorghastrum nutans- Bouteloua curtipendula-Andropogon gerardii*, and the *Leptochloa dubia* subtypes. Old stands of *Panicum virgatum* were common on mesic sites that now contain near monotypic stands of switchgrass. The *Sorghastrum nutans-Bouteloua curtipendula-Andropogon gerardii* subtype is prevalent on upland sites and some stands still have high concentrations of smooth brome or can have mixtures of native tall grasses. In 2005, one restored field was inadvertently seeded with green sprangletop (*Leptochloa dubia*), which was the dominant grass at the time of the field survey. On the color infrared imagery this type appeared as a mottled light pink with a fair amount of blue-green undertones. Some of the fields still showed signs of past plowing.

Photo Signature Examples

Representative Ground Photo

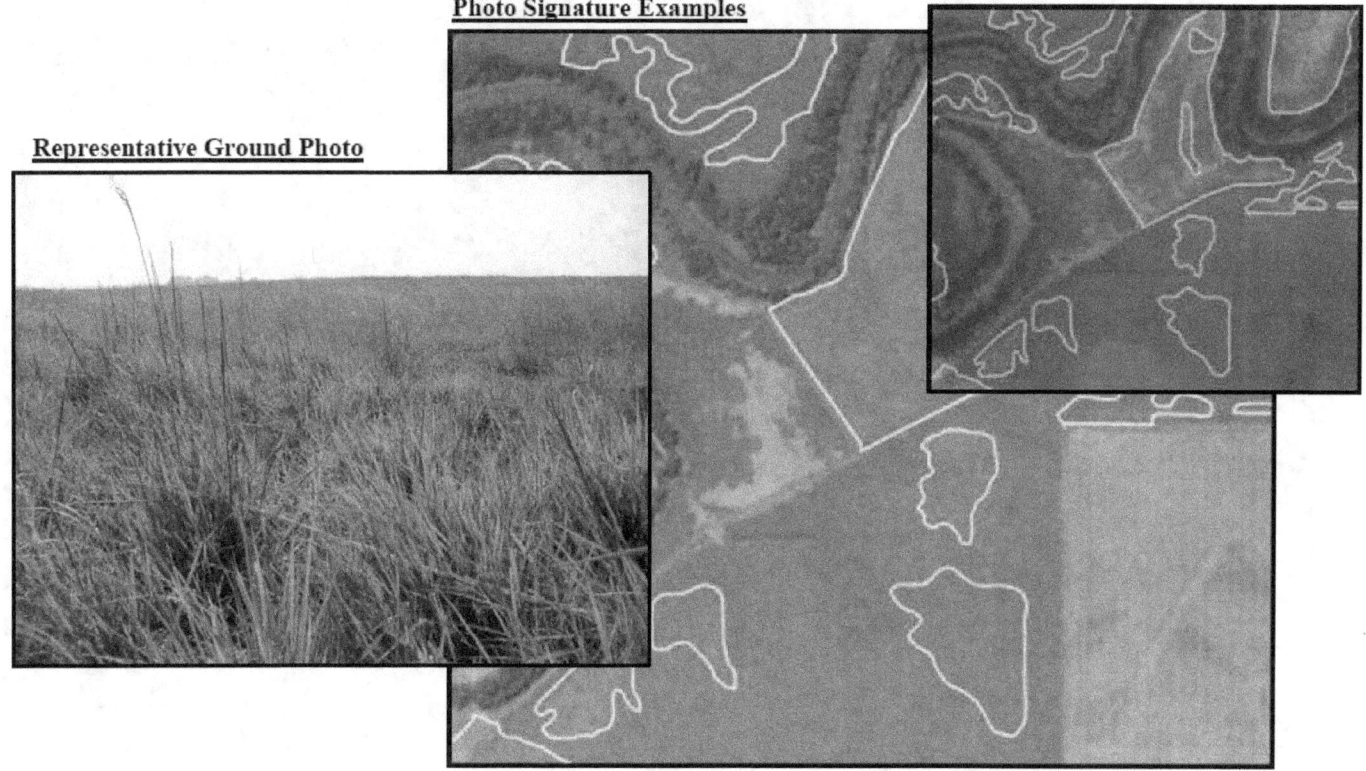

H-OFLD   Old Field Weedy Herbaceous Vegetation

Associations and Alliances

Common Species
Conium maculatum
Kochia scoparia
Bromus japonicus
Rumex altissimus
Ambrosia psilostachya
Bromus inermis
Bromus tectorum
Andropogon gerardii
Pascopyrum smithii

Range and Distribution

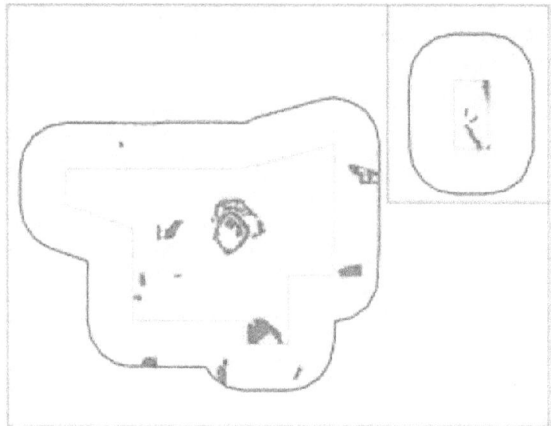

Description

This type represents disturbed areas at FOLS including the historic dump site, the oxbow island, and the low-lying areas along the Pawnee River floodplain. The vegetation for this site was highly variable but was generally dominated by mid-height introduced grasses (0.5 m) and tall annual forbs (to 2 m). Local patches may have contained small early successional trees (such as *Gleditsia triacanthos*) and native grasses (including *Andropogon gerardii*, *Pascopyrum smithii*, and *Sporobolus asper*). This type usually had a high percentage of annual species cover (> 30%) and a high percentage of forb cover relative to surrounding fields mapped as either smooth brome or restored grassland. Depending on the species composition three subtypes were identified at FOLS. These included: *Conium maculatum* Subtype (Poison Hemlock Subtype), *Kochia scoparia* Subtype (Mexican Firebush Subtype) and Fine Mosaic Subtype. In the GIS layer, stands of this type that contained a clear dominant were noted by including the dominant species in the Dom_Mod attribute field. However since most are annual early seral species, locations of these subtypes are not expected to remain constant. On the true color imagery this type had a highly variable signature ranging from dark green splotches (lush vegetation) to a mottled tan and grey (sparse, dry vegetation).

Photo Signature Examples

Representative Ground Photo

H-SMBR   *Bromus inermis* Semi-natural Herbaceous Alliance
Smooth Brome Semi-natural Herbaceous Alliance

Associations and Alliances
Bromus inermis Semi-natural Herbaceous Alliance

Common Species
Bromus inermis
Pascopyrum smithii
Stipa comata
Convolvulus arvense
Kochia scoparia
Setaria pumila

Range and Distribution

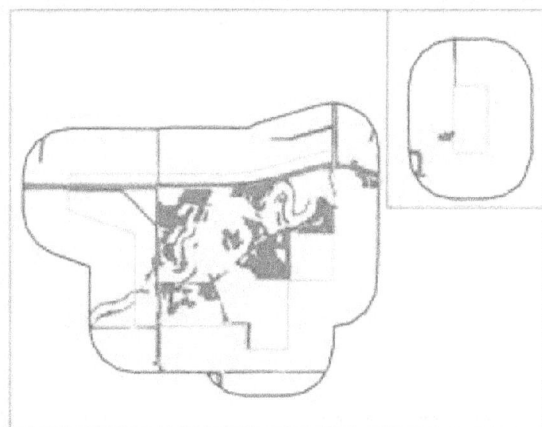

Description
This type is common to the area in and around Fort Larned, where it dominates the areas formerly used for agriculture. This grass was likely seeded extensively for pasture and hay production. Smooth brome is also common in the restored prairie and old field map units but in these situations it was usually not the dominant. Stands of this type usually had little diversity other than a handful of other non-native forbs. Typically smooth brome grows about 0.3 to 1 m tall, and entirely covers more than 90% of the plots. Native grasses cover less than 10% of these stands, but can include *Bouteloua curtipendula*, *Sorghastrum nutans* and *Andropogon gerardii*. At FOLS this type is being actively managed through herbicide treatments and prairie restoration efforts. On the color infrared imagery this type had a characteristic smooth, pink signature that sometimes contained dark red splotches with the presence of weedy forbs.

Photo Signature Examples

Representative Ground Photos

H-SMRT   Hydrologically Disturbed Seasonal *Polygonum* Vegetation
Smartweed species Seasonally Flooded Herbaceous Alliance

Associations and Alliances
Hydrologically Disturbed Seasonal *Polygonum* Vegetation

Common Species
Polygonum lapathifolium
Polygonum bicorne
Conium maculatum
Rumex altissimus

Range and Distribution

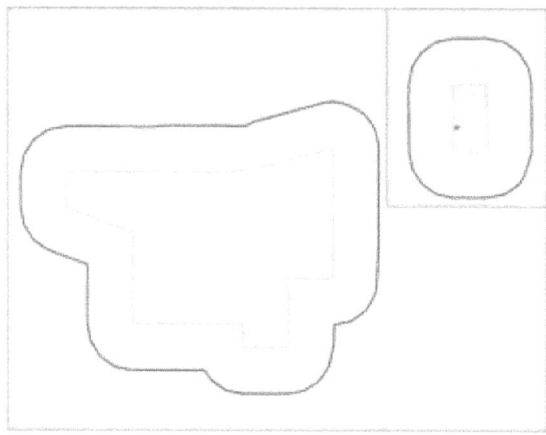

Description
This type occurs in two distinct areas, along the Pawnee River bottom in the main unit of Fort Larned National Historic Site and where a small drainage has been impounded by the roadbed on the west side of the remote Santa Fe Trail Ruts Site. Due to the timing of the imagery only the site at the Ruts Site was mapped. The extensive stands in the Pawnee River are seasonal and this stream was filled with water when the imagery was acquired. Damming of the Pawnee River upstream and downstream from FOLS has led to silt accumulation and seasonal standing water in the river bed. Water depth can vary from 0 to 1 m. Depending on the water depth and clarity, smartweed vegetation can be found seasonally in all but the deepest channel of the river bed. Basically the whole river corridor mapped as Streams / River could be mapped as this type. At the Ruts Site, there is little bare ground or standing water. Other than a few annual sunflowers (*Helianthus annuus*) along the fence, the vegetation is less than 1 m. tall.

Photo Signature Examples

Representative Ground Photo

H-WTWG   *Pascopyrum smithii* Herbaceous Alliance
Western Wheatgrass Herbaceous Alliance

Associations and Alliances
Pascopyrum smithii Herbaceous Alliance

Common Species
Pascopyrum smithii
Bromus japonicus
Bromus inermis

Range and Distribution

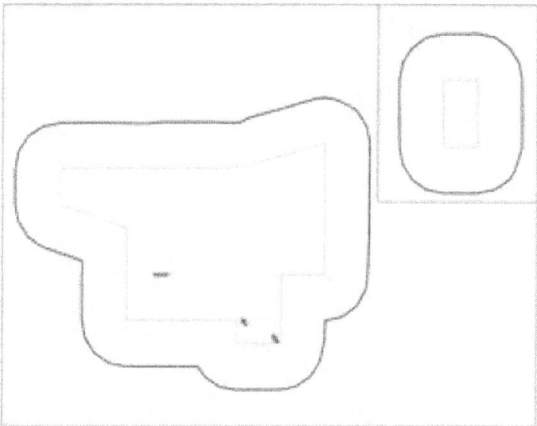

Description
This type had a fairly restricted distribution at FOLS consisting of three polygons and due to its small extent was only sampled with an observation point. This type occurred primarily on dry soils and contained other non-native herbaceous species. On the true color imagery this type appeared similar to the other grassland types, which may have led to some confusion in the mapping. Its signature was usually light green and tan. More sampling of this type would help better define its distribution and species composition.

Photo Signature Examples

Representative Ground Photo

H-JOHN   *Sorghum halepense* Herbaceous Alliance
Johnsongrass Herbaceous Alliance

Associations and Alliances
Sorghum halepense Herbaceous Alliance

Common Species
Sorghum halepense

Range and Distribution

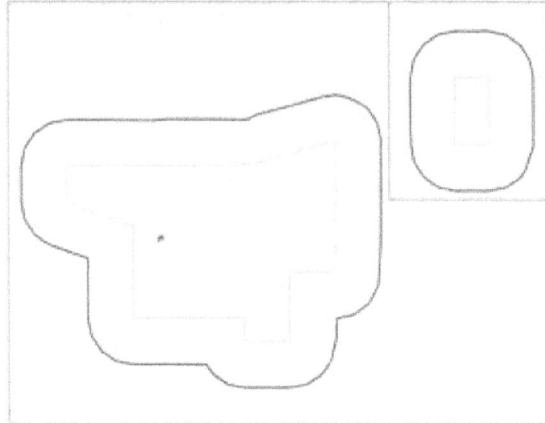

Description
This type represents one area at Fort Larned that was dominated by Johnsongrass and primarily surrounded by native prairie restoration and smooth brome stands. This type formed a dense, lush stand that was over 0.5 meter tall. On the true color imagery this type appeared as light green grasslands. This type had a similar signature to other grasslands and some confusion may have occurred in the mapping of this type.

Photo Signature Examples

Representative Ground Photo

APPENDIX G: Final FOLS Vegetation Map

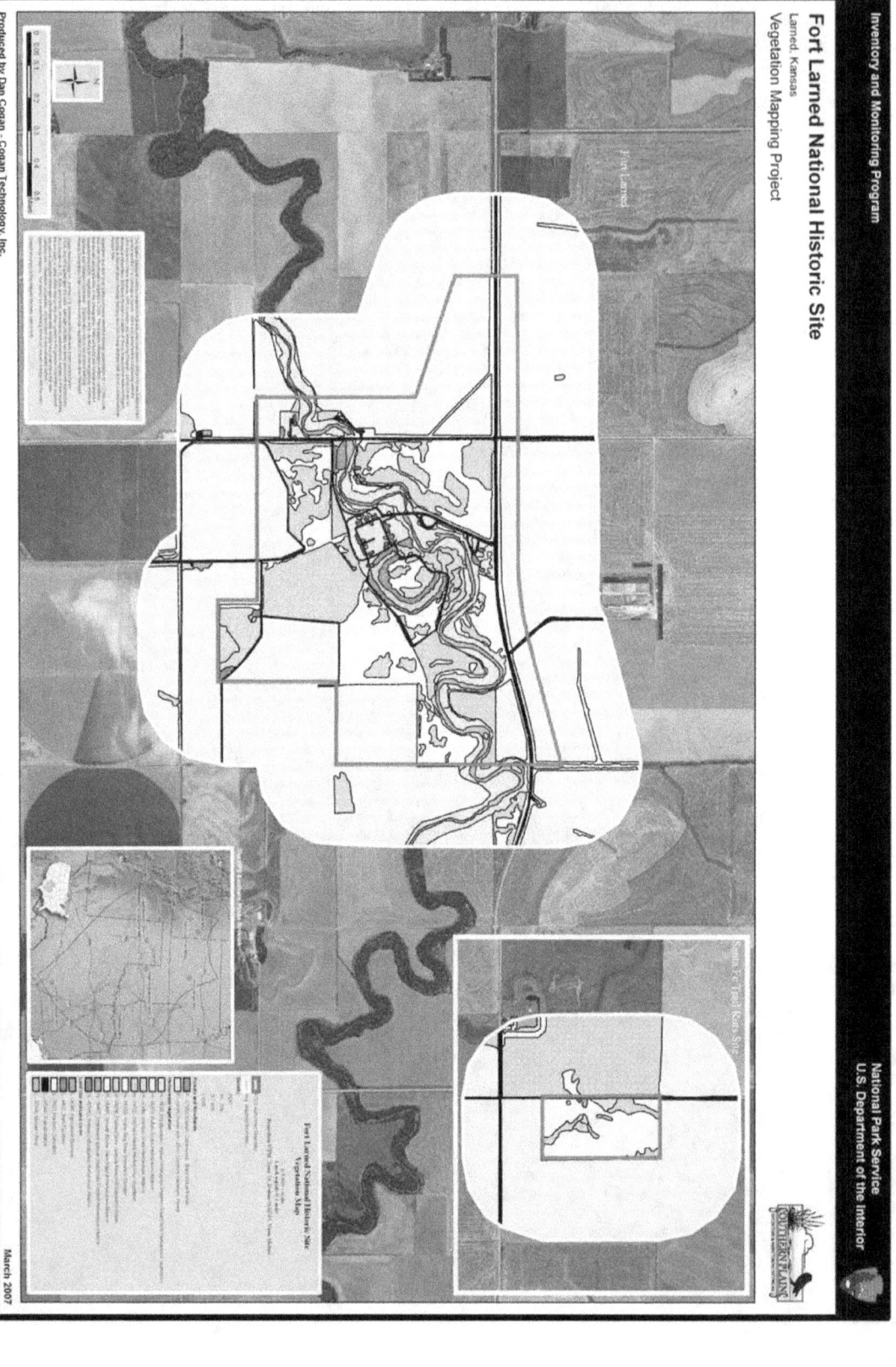

Fort Larned National Historic Site

Larned, Kansas
Vegetation Mapping Project

Produced by Dan Cogan - Cogan Technology, Inc.

March 2007

NPS D-66, May 2007

National Park Service
U.S. Department of the Interior

Southern Plains Inventory and Monitoring Network
P.O. Box 329 (mailing)
100 Ladybird Lane (physical)
Johnson City, TX 78636

www.nps.gov

EXPERIENCE YOUR AMERICA ™